# ENTERPRISE COMPLIANCE MANAGEMENT
# (ECM)

# ENTERPRISE COMPLIANCE MANAGEMENT (ECM)

## BRINGING INFLUENCES TOGETHER

### A PRAGMATIC GUIDE FOR ATTAINING COMPLIANCE ACROSS THE ENTERPRISE

*James J. Finnegan*

iUniverse, Inc.
New York  Lincoln  Shanghai

Enterprise Compliance Management (ECM)
Bringing Influences Together

iUniverse, Inc.

For information address:
iUniverse, Inc.
2021 Pine Lake Road, Suite 100
Lincoln, NE 68512
www.iuniverse.com

ISBN: 0-595-32372-3

Printed in the United States of America

# Contents

# Acknowledgement

A small cadre of individuals and organizations has been involved in the creation of this Guide. They have provided guidance, constructive criticism, and support through the substantial number of revisions and refinements of this Guide.

Dave Bauman—United States
Dave graduated from the University of Illinois, Urbana with a BSIE and the Stuart School of Business IIT with an MBA. He has spent more than thirty-five years in Operations, Total Quality, Engineering, Research and Development, Distribution/Materials Planning and ERP systems implementation. Dave has worked in a number of cultures in Europe and South America. He currently lives in South Texas and is Vice President of High Volume Engineering, Quality and Distribution for a major manufacturing firm.

Jeremy Cole—BEng—United Kingdom
Jeremy specialized in Systems Analysis at University, quickly moving into the Manufacturing Industry, working in the Quality Assurance arena. He then moved into the Service Sector via the Construction Industry. Having worked for both the public and private sectors, Jeremy is currently involved in HSQE in the rail industry.

Alastair Duggin—BEng, MSc, CEng.—United Kingdom
Alastair has been involved in systems for many years in Australia, Hong Kong, and the UK as a Consultant and as IS Manager. He has worked in several industries as well as in the public sector. Further information is available at www.DugginSystems.co.uk.

Norman Willoughby—ABEng—Canada
Norman has planned and managed a wide sectoral variety of projects as a consultant to industry and government, as an entrepreneur, and as a government project officer. His experience covers a diversity of work environments in more than a dozen countries. He is the author of several management books, including "Incredibly Easy Project Management," published in the UK by Management Books 2000 Ltd.

Pallas-Athena (www.Pallas-Athena.com) for
providing a copy of the Protos Business Process Management suite to assist in the
creation of illustrations for this Guide.

European Foundation for Quality Management (EFQM; www.efqm.org) for allowing an interpretation of EFQM material to be used as a Business Influence example.

Proforma Corporation (www.proformacorp.com) for providing a copy of the ProVision Business Process Management suite to assist in the creation of illustrations for this Guide.

# Introduction

My first understanding of the disastrous effects of noncompliance occurred during my life as a manufacturing production planner. I had load-leveled the production line, taking particular delight in the assurance that the plant's most critical work center was operating at optimum level.

When I arrived for work the following day I looked out the first floor planning room window at the critical work center just below. What should have been gratification soon turned to dismay. During the graveyard shift a great pile of in-process product had accumulated in front of the critical work center; its large machine lay in parts all over the floor. I quickly negotiated the stairs to the production floor and was in front of the disarray within minutes, outwardly pleading for an explanation.

The maintenance manager looked at me as if I was crazy. "What's the matter kid?" he inquired.

"Oh, nothing," I said sarcastically, "you've just shut down the plant and the end of month production output has gone down the tubes. What are you guys playing at?"

"Look kid," he said, "I am required to take this machine out of service every 2,000 hours for a complete overhaul. It has run over 2,000 hours and that is what I am doing. Those are the safety rules and I am sticking by them. Now get out of my people's way so they can get their job done."

It was then I fully realized that the effects of unknown and competing compliance requirements could be disastrous. I had complied with the Master Schedule in an effort to get the product out the door. Maintenance had complied with the safety regulations. The result was a full shift of production was lost, something I heard about for sometime thereafter. The problem was we were both right. The company, however, suffered as a result.

During the following five years, I graduated into materials and operations management, expanding my appreciation for the variety and increasing number of conflicting compliance requirements affecting the business. Some of these were simply influences, requiring consideration when making a decision or completing a process. Others were requirements with significant impacts. I consolidated them under the heading of Business Influences in an effort to try and simplify matters. Either way they seemed to be overwhelming, inundating every second of my day.

As time passed, I took on a project manager's role within Information Technology, hailed as a "reward" for my implementation and optimization of production systems. My task was to implement, in one year's time, a global materials system for the company. The project, completed on time, was not without an appreciation for an additional suite of influencing requirements, each demanding varying and many times conflicting priorities.

It was then that I started to look for ways to accommodate the ever-increasing number of influences that surrounded me. I would often sketch compliance models on whiteboards, but since there was no software available to help with automation, they were soon out of date. That was almost thirty years ago, and it is only in the last several years that I have felt that there are sufficient application software capabilities available to help the consumer practitioner deal with what may seem to be a daunting task.

I have often compared the mapping of high-level business influence requirements to the picture on a jigsaw box cover. Many times people become overwhelmed with the pile of pieces, the detail, put off by what they see as an overwhelming task. However, once there is an appreciation of the overall picture, the play of the pieces becomes much easier to plan.

Over the years, I have created a Guide to assist me in addressing the effects of compliance inundation. The Guide has taken many forms. However, this is the first formal edition of what I anticipate to be a continuous process. I see it as an evolutionary effort, refining its concepts as influence variants change and supporting application software advances. The Guide is comprised of five sections:

1 An overview of the Enterprise Compliance Management concept.

2 The Guide itself, which addresses the three fundamental environments: Reference, Infrastructure, and Compliance, and the implementation thereof.

3 Lessons Learned: a series of examples from my work history that have substantiated the need for the Guide and have helped in the refinement of its concepts.

4 A conclusion reviewing the important ideas expressed in the commentary.

5 Appendices containing specific examples supporting the concepts herein, help on where to go for further information, and a section addressing semantics—my definitions of the words and concepts used in this work.

I hope this guide will help you as much as it assisted me in efforts to assure businesses that all Business Influence requirements are identified, translated to the business and a supporting process and their complying product are provided. This is the key to Enterprise Compliance Management.

Your comments and suggestions are invited. Please send them to JJJF@TheECM.Com or visit the book's website at www.TheECM.com .

# Overview

Compliance has long been associated with legislation and regulations. However, when one thinks about it we are required to comply with some requirement in everything we do, such as obeying speed restrictions, completing tax returns, and the like. Business complicates matters by adding another layer of compliance requirements to our lives, and it is this challenge that we address in this Guide.

Compliance Requirements present themselves in a variety of forms. At the highest level, for the purposes of this Guide, we can refer to compliance requirements as Business Influences created or received by management, customers, suppliers, or competitors. The creation of a Compliance Model is an excellent way to document Business Influencers and Influences. See an example of a Compliance Model in *Figure 1*. The model provides a high-level view of the requirements for compliance on a single sheet of paper or webpage, making it easier to convey the number of Influences that affect a business as well as to the influencers who supply the requirements.

The central focus of the Compliance Model is the Influence Management function. Influence Management's task is to assure the identification of all Business Influence requirements, their translation to the business, and the provision of supporting processes and complying products. The management of Influence Management itself is a process (See a summary of the overall administrative process in *Figure 2*) providing the necessary assurance that the influences are properly administered.

One of the most beneficial results of this effort is the creation of a hierarchical structure of scenarios and processes that operate and help optimize the business. Another is the identification of the Business Functions that provide a suite of capabilities supporting all aspects of the business. Once the initiation of the Influence Management evolution has taken place, the composition and organization of these functions may differ from traditional lines. An Influence Management oriented organization example is shown in *Figure 4*. You can see that the focus is on Influence Management as the key to attaining continuing compliance management.

Enterprise Compliance Management (ECM), with Influence Management at its core, focuses on a holistic, top-down, business oriented view of compliance. The ECM Guide discusses a common sense method for the creation and management—with the use of integrated software applications—of compliance on an enterprise basis.

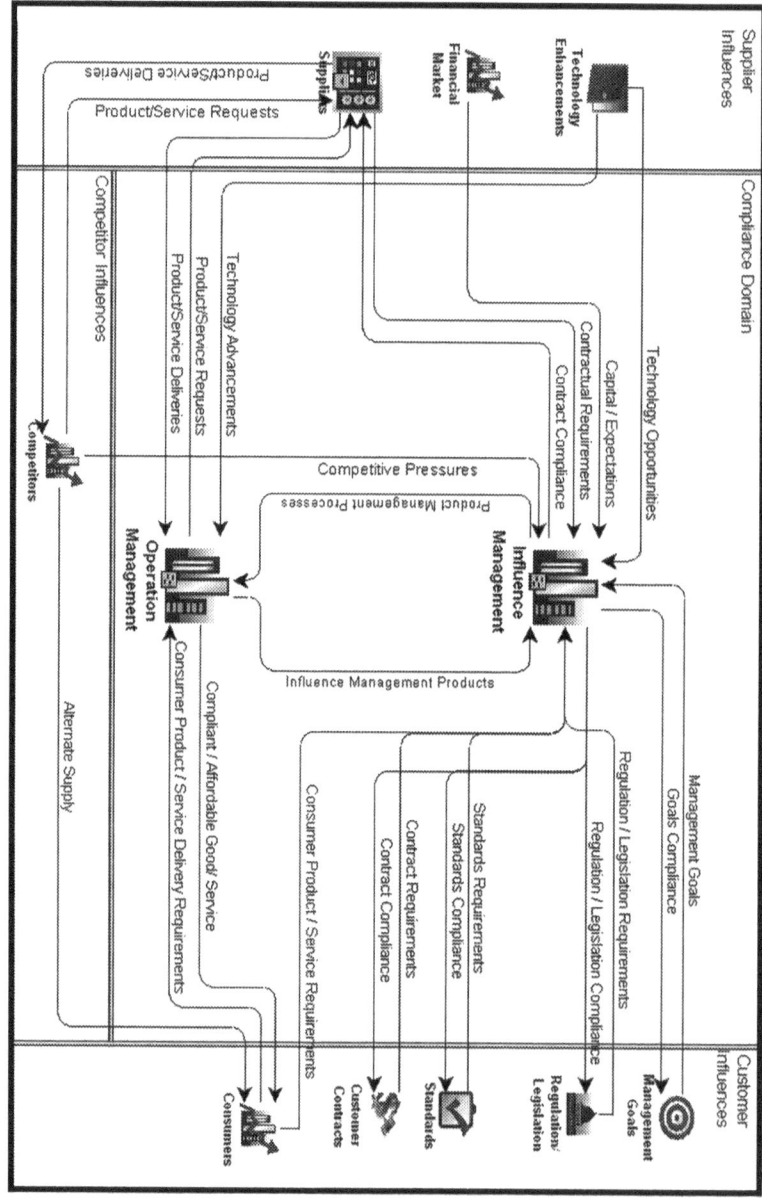

*Figure 1—Compliance Model Example*

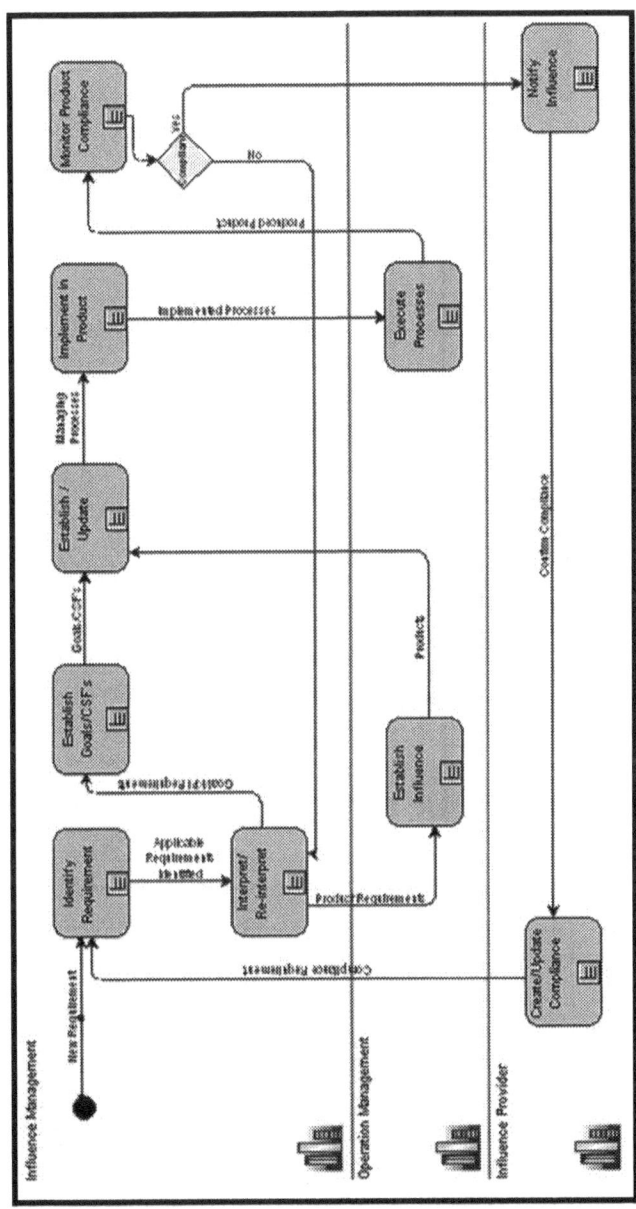

*Figure 2—Influence Management Process Overview Example*

ECM begins by addressing Influence Requirements and the creation of a Compliance Model. It continues with the creation of the Reference, Infrastructure, and Compliance environments utilized to support the model and facilitate continuing compliance. (See *Figure 3, Structure Overview*)

The Reference Environment is the repository that provides a baseline of information. It contains, as a minimum, information related to Business Influences and Scenarios, Function Scenarios, the Organization Model, and a variety of Elemental Information in the form of Data, Applications, and Content. In short, it becomes the knowledge repository of the business.

The Infrastructure Environment supports the repositories that hold the Reference information and provides the process automation to update and manage them. The Business Process Library, Portals, and Process Automation are examples of the capabilities provided by the infrastructure environment.

The ECM Guide does not address the specific use of application software to help attain Enterprise Compliance Management. However, it does refer to generic types of supporting software as appropriate. See *Appendix D, Information Providers,* for an illustrative list of professional bodies that can provide application product information.

The Compliance Environment utilizes the Reference & Infrastructure Environments to manage information links to standards, contracts, legislation, management requirements, etc. In addition, it manages the compliance processes and their related products, assuring closed-loop compliance feedback.

As part of the description of ECM, this Guide addresses its implementation. The sequence of implementation (See *Figure 5, Steps to Compliance*) is the result of several years of effort spent developing a simple yet comprehensive approach to the implementation of continuing compliance within a business enterprise environment. An abundance of opportunity examples, some of which are discussed in the *Lessons Learned* section, provided valuable input to that effort.

One final comment before we begin. Picture a board director with a copy of the business' Compliance Model in front of him or her while you are pitching an initiative that supports the requirements of one or more of the Business Influences. If the board understands the model and its implications, think of how much simpler it would be for both of you to form a conclusion regarding your initiative. Without a Compliance Model yours is yet another point solution, the total ramifications of which may be unknown and could very well be detrimental to the success of the business as a whole.

# The ECM Guide

## Compliance

### Requirement to Comply

We receive requirements, and provide requirements to others, in the form of messages. In fact, most of the effort we expend in life is spent on either attempting to convey a requirement message to someone or something (e.g., a data entry screen) or trying to be compliant with, or in some cases ignore, a requirements message that we have received. Messages requiring compliance are everywhere; they are part of our everyday lives. Traffic control signs, ever-changing flight and train timetables, system maintenance, alerts, social commitments, are but a few examples. The growing number of messages over an increasing variety of media (e-mail, fax, voice, text messages, etc.) may very well be stealing the precious little free time we have for ourselves.

Business further complicates matters by adding an additional layer of requirements messages (regulations, standards, management requests, etc.) to an already overwhelming situation. Dealing with the increasing number of messages would be effective if we all had a facilitating environment in place to manage them. Sadly, many individuals and businesses have not allocated the time or the resources essential to the implementation of a suitable facilitating environment. As a result, the management of requirements message inundation has become increasingly ineffective.

In addition to the confusion caused by inundation, compliance to a requirement is often difficult to define. The situation is made even more difficult while we continue to manage the ever-changing needs of our business (and our lives) and their often conflicting demands. The administrative costs associated with attempting to maintain compliance within this ever-changing environment tend to grow exponentially.

What must happen? It is a matter of fundamentals. Continuous compliance is everyone's business, and must not be relegated to the Compliance Officer. Even if there is one he or she are usually in a reactive mode addressing symptoms, leaving little time to address the problems. All members of the organization, in one form or other, are required to comply. Individuals must be continuously compliant with the requirements of their own business environment. Managers also must be continuously compliant with the requirements of their own business functions. At the highest level, companies and their directors must be continuously compliant with the variety of requirements set down by influencers. Indeed, if all requirements and management decisions are included, continuous compliance management becomes the optimized management of the business.

The benefits of continuous compliance manifest themselves in two major ways:

1. Effort Reduction—There will be a reduction in effort in the business consistent with the creation of a continuous compliance culture. You must know what to do and how to do it, understand why you must accomplish tasks as prescribed, and understand the detrimental effects on the business if you are non-compliant. Equally important, you must continuously review your environment with an eye to optimizing the compliance relationships with Influencers.

2. Effort Avoidance—Another result of the creation of a continuous compliance culture between the business and Influencers is the minimization of the need for external organizations to conduct validity checks to assure compliance. I do not know how many times I have seen the result of non-compliance addressed with audit upon audit, attacking the symptoms, not the problem, and leaving destruction in their wake. One good example is taking one expensive physical inventory after another resulting in a variety of unfounded variances while ignoring the lax transaction procedures and broken processes that caused the problem in the first place.

Therefore, messages and expanding media inundation lead to increased effort and decreased productivity, and in many cases result in ineffective communication. Employees' time becomes focused on busy-work rather than business growth activities when it should be the other way around. Think of it, with compliance management in place you might actually get some productive work accomplished.

## Causes of Inundation

There are a number of possible causes for inundation. The following are some illustrative examples.

a. Business Influences are not defined, nor are they translated to the business—Many businesses focus on the operational running of the business while influences that affect the business are either obscured or totally forgotten. Business Influences (contracts, core values, standards, etc.) are often not defined, nor are they translated to Influence Management or Operation Processes. As a result, Business Influences may not play an integral part in their day-to-day operations. This lack of clear direction causes increased uncertainty, which, in turn, increases the need for continual clarification of information. The obvious result is an increase in inquiry messages and consequent confirmation messages as well as efforts to try to compensate for a broken Information Supply Chain.

I was once involved with a company who had a primary performance contract based upon specific criteria. The company could be prosperous or severely fined for lack of proper performance. Of interest was the fact that those same criteria were not part of the contracts let to the subcontractors providing the services that fulfilled the company's contract. Attention to translation detail goes a long way to helping a business remain prosperous, unless your company has the luxury of being bailed out by the taxpayer.

b. Business Processes are not defined or derived from Business Influences and/or Scenarios or competently performed—During the past several years, there has been an overwhelming effort by businesses to document their processes. The results of the significant effort expended on what is often a bottom-up approach may very well be totally at odds with the way the Business Influences may dictate the business should be operating. Frequently, this is due to Business Influences not identified or translated to Influence Management or Operation Functions.

The bottom-up process definition may also suffer from the constituent's or consultancy's lack of competence in "best practice" techniques. This could create less than optimal process content and configuration. Many industries tend to have parochial views of their environment. Often one hears that a certain industry is "different and complex." These cloistered views often prevent the industry from sharing best practice with other industries because "the others don't understand," when in fact the difference in many cases is nothing more than semantics. You must research "Best Practice" content to assure that it is applicable to and supportive of your requirements. By doing your homework you will avoid the pitfalls of inappropriate practices or those which are simply the "Best" your consultancy's "Practice" can manage.

Additionally, the utilization of the business system and technology capabilities may hinder the constituent. For example, many business systems or modules, purchased for the best of reasons, immediately become "shelf-ware" and are never installed or implemented. Others, due to inefficient or ineffective efforts resulting in "scope crimp," are "implemented" but do not provide the originally marketed and agreed upon results. This often happens when there is considerable consumption of resource (time, effort, and funds) on "that feel good factor" by the supporting consultancy or the attempted "transfer of risk" by management during the preparation stages of major systems' implementation. These efforts leave precious few resources with which to complete the task, and the result is "scope crimp." Examples of these are available in the *Lessons Learned* section of this Guide.

However, sometimes the constituents' lack of competence is outside their control due to the absence of best practice techniques, and/or the provided system and technology capabilities may not support their requirements.

c. Business Automation may be either fragmented and/or unable to handle exceptions—Overall, organizations spend a considerable amount of time, effort, and money defining business processes with a view to optimizing their business and therefore the management of exceptions. Often, the supporting business system's capabilities are either fragmented and/or unable to handle these exceptions. When this happens, the optimizing initiative slows and often halts. Automation, in the form of Work Flow engines, Document Management and the like, provide mediums that facilitate feedback from exception-driven processes, creating outputs through dynamic task activity monitoring which can be utilized to gauge compliance with the requirements of the Business Influences.

At one time in my career, I was challenged with an opportunity involving the distribution of drawings to maintenance personal on a worldwide basis. What was a manual, time-consuming, courier involved effort became an automated on-line response system providing timely and user specified information when they needed it. Workflow automated the gaps in the then current business system application software suite saving the company time, money and increasing customer satisfaction.

## The Role of the Message

Requirements for compliance move from sender to receiver in the form of messages. Therefore, in most cases a Message should be structured data passed from sender to receiver via Message Media (document, fax, e-mail, website, electronic sign, etc.). Messages can occur between people; the most common message is a conversation or discussion. They can occur between people and Media;

a good example of this is the individual entering information into a business system. They can also occur within and between Media, the result of internal business system workflow or interfaces between business systems, e.g., EDI, EFT, etc.

## Message Categories

There are three categories of Messages.

1. Transactions—Transaction messages are very structured and usually associated with a transaction-based business system. For the most part these messages are part of off-the-shelf business systems packages and are generally, within certain limits, configurable.

2. Action—Action Messages are semi-structured and require the execution of a task. These messages tend to be the compensating factor for the lack of translation between the Business Influences, the Business Scenarios/Processes, and the inability of the business systems and technology to cope with influence requirements. Action messages therefore further augment the expansion of an even more effort-centric environment. These messages are clearly symptoms of the opportunities for process optimization and probable automation.

3. Information—Information Messages are unstructured and may require no further business process-related action. Examples of these are carbon copies and blind carbon copies in memos, e-mails, and other media. In reality, these messages tend to be confused with Action Messages and very often consume a considerable amount of time and effort to process.

Each of these categories affects the business in varying degrees. Obviously, the more a business can implement transaction type messages, the leaner it will be.

## Message Media

Messages are different from Media because messages convey what is said while Media defines how it is managed and delivered. There are two types of media:

1. Message Delivery Media—Examples of this media are telephone, fax, e-mail, websites, etc. This media generally requires a minimum of information and structure to support the transmission of messages. Often, only the address of the receiver is required. Because of this unstructured environment, receivers often spend a significant amount of time trying to decipher requirement(s) from many of the messages they receive.

2. Message Management Media—Examples of this media are Business Systems, Workflow, Business Process Management, etc.—media that help provide a structured environment in which messages are processed. However, this environment also can be plagued with fruitless, unnecessary, and wasted effort if not managed in a competent manner and supported by robust infrastructure.

Depending upon the situation and the capabilities at hand, a variety of users may utilize several types of media to deliver and/or manage a specific type of message. For example, a new sales order may be transmitted by fax from a remote sales office; or emailed and picked up by workflow and entered directly into a system; or entered directly into order entry by a data entry clerk; or moved by electronic data interchange between the customer's and business's system. It is important when defining requirements messages that one initially concentrates on the message, separating it from the variety of available and sometimes confusing media options.

## Why is a Message important?

Those of you who have seen military action or held an equally critical role in business know the importance of getting the message across. A famous message was once passed verbally through the trenches and corrupted from "Send reinforcements, we're going to advance" to "Send two and sixpence, we're going to a dance". The proper transmission and interpretation of a message may mean life or death to individuals or to a company so it is important to get it right the first time.

The most effective way to communicate is to establish closed-loop processes that provide the sender with the knowledge that the intended receiver (be that another person or media) has:

1. Received a Message;
2. Read the Message;
3. Understood the Message or made an appropriate inquiry; and very importantly,
4. Acted appropriately and delivered the product requested.

Effective message requirements management is pivotal to insuring the receipt of messages, the understanding of their content, and the return of the appropriate product. Only then does the sender know that he or she has achieved compliance. With effective requirements message management, there is a reduction in the inundation of messages and associated effort. This closed loop environment increases the effectiveness of messages and helps to assure compliance with requirements.

## The Need for Requirements Message Management

The management of requirements messages is paramount to the effective utilization of one's time. The identification of the correct message for a given Business Influence, the infrastructure which supports it, the competence with which it is delivered, and the effectiveness with which it is handled are all part of Enterprise Compliance Management. ECM is the medium that provides end-to-end management and optimization of messaging within any organization. Where may it be utilized, you might ask. Just look for the following symptoms:

a. Paper—Paper is often the most obvious, especially where there tends to be a lot of it. A quick walk through your business will soon highlight areas that need attention. However, there may be a number of reasons for a pile of paper: The person responsible may be disorganized or in a constrained work center and there is no way the amount of work demanded can be handled; or the process, system, and/or the technology environment within which a person works may be deficient.

   I am reminded of a plant tour I took a month after the millennium. The company had implemented a new ERP system to handle the year 2000. The system was implemented at great expense and with much fanfare. The result was increased paperwork to compensate for the lack of joined-up processes that should have been implemented as part of the "success". The company, needless to say, now had to enlist the same or another consultancy to address the flawed implementation.

b. Messages—Messages are abundant. However, not all messages are on paper. Some arrive in the form of e-mail, a telephone call, a comment from over the cubicle divider, alerts and/or notifications arriving from a business system, etc. Many individuals are overwhelmed with messages, so much so that they can concentrate on little else. Sometimes there are so many that the individuals cannot get their work done and do not have time to answer all the messages they have received. On inspection, one might even find that many of the messages are duplicates, follow-ups caused by the lack of response to previously unanswered messages.

c. Media—Individuals and businesses have many types of media at their disposal. Sometimes they will utilize several of them in an attempt to try to get the message across. Take for example the memo that has to reach every member of the sales force. This experience has happened to me on more than one occasion. First, the memo was e-mailed, then it was faxed, and finally it was sent out in the interoffice mail to ensure delivery to everyone. Use of more than one medium to send a message increases the effort required to deal with the backlog created.

Shoveling sand against the sea is the action I have in mind when placed in these situations. The harder I try, the worse it becomes, and the effort-associated frustration finally boils over and I get close to suffering "burn-out." Obviously, all these symptoms manifest the need to focus attention on the management of messages.

## What are your options?

There are really only two options:

1. Trying to accommodate by living with the increasing inundation is not a realistic option for anyone intending to stay on top of the incoming flow. The expanding audience combined with the ever-increasing capabilities of media able to deliver and receive more messages—and faster—will thwart your attempts to be effective.
2. Effective Messages Management is the only way one will survive.

However, this is easy enough to say, but how is it accomplished? Option 2 is what this work is about, a Guide to help attain a state of requirements message compliance, benefit the business instead of bogging it down with busy-work, and most importantly, better the quality of business life.

The Enterprise Compliance Management (ECM) Guide facilitates the effective, competent, and compliant identification and translation of requirements messages to processes and products delivered by optimized message media.

## What does it mean to the Business?

The successful implementation of ECM results in the following benefits:

1. Identification of Opportunities—During the creation of the Compliance Environment, it is easy to identify opportunities for streamlining Business

and Function Scenarios and Processes. This often leads to a redistribution and/or reduction in effort across the enterprise.

2. A Single Version of the Truth—The Compliance Environment provides a single, online, and up-to-date version of the truth that reduces exceptions and delays caused by inconsistent or unavailable information. This is a key element in the effectiveness of Compliance.

3. Establishing Compliance—Processes translated from documented Business Influences and Business and Function Scenarios ensure a complete hierarchy of compliance governance across functions.

4. Competence and Effective Use—The assurance that the business makes competent and effective use of the infrastructure capabilities. This keeps the business lean and helps it attain a competitive edge in the marketplace. There are many examples of ineffective use—all one has to do is review all the business systems ineffectively implemented. The system may have been implemented "on-time and on-budget," but is it effective and competently used? Think again, when you review some of these examples in the Lessons Learned section of this guide.

# ECM Structure Overview

ECM is comprised of three supporting environments, which, when properly created and maintained, enable the enterprise to manage its continuing compliance requirements. See *Figure 3* for a pictorial overview of the structure.

The Reference Environment is the repository that provides a baseline of information for continuing compliance. It contains information relating to the Business Influences, Business Scenarios, Function Scenarios, the Organization Model, and Elemental Information in the form of Data, Content, Applications, etc.

The Infrastructure Environment supports the repositories that hold the Reference information and facilitates their update and management. The Business Process Library, Portals, and Process Automation are examples of facilities provided by the infrastructure environment.

The Compliance Environment utilizes the Reference & Infrastructure Environments along with the Compliance Model and its processes and products to establish the structure with which to manage compliance.

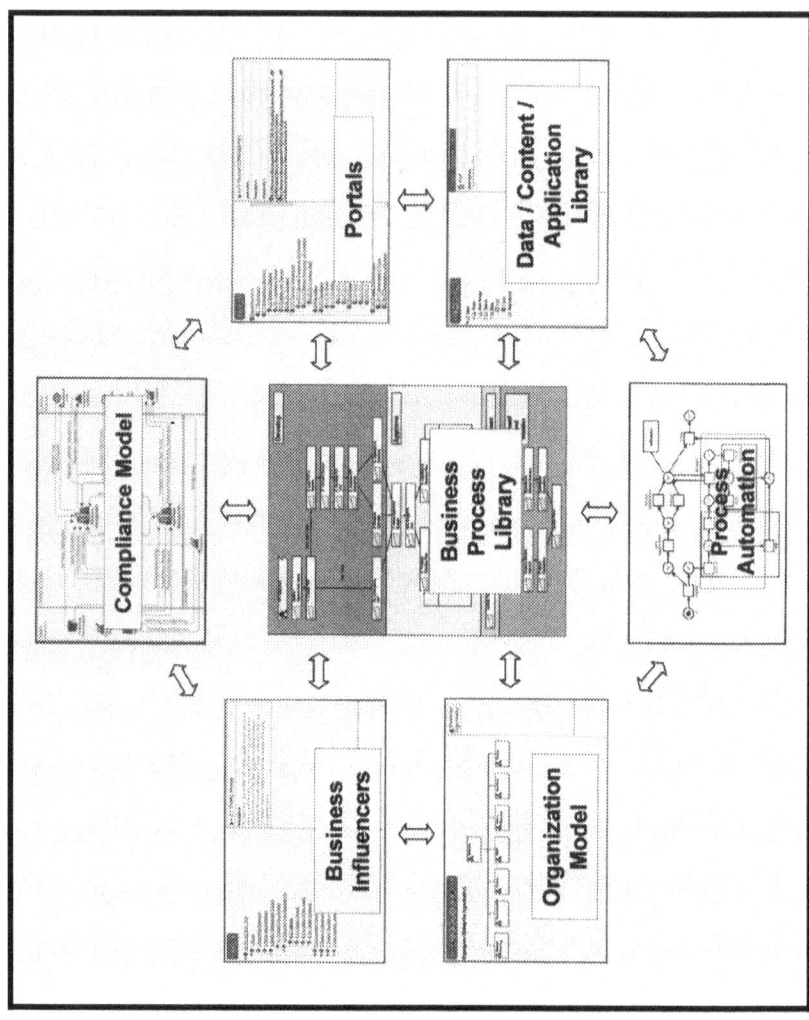

*Figure 3—Structure Overview*

# The Reference Environment

The Reference Environment provides one of the foundations for the implementation and continuing success of ECM. This environment is the repository for Business Influences, Business Scenarios, Business Functions and Scenarios, the Organization Model, and Elemental Information. A review of each of these topics follows.

## Business Influences

Business Influences are the reasons for being in business and may greatly affect the way the business operates. The difficulty, of course, is identifying which influence affects the business, the extent to which it affects the business, and the extent to which one influence may affect another influence, causing differences in priorities within the business. Business Influences may take many forms. See *Appendix A* for some additional detail. The following are a few examples:

a.  Standards—Standards are the benchmarks to which an enterprise may aspire, and/or be required to conform or comply. ISO, EFQM, ITIL, GAAP, etc., are examples of such standards.

b.  Contracts—Contracts are agreements between the business and customers and/or suppliers. They will certainly have a significant impact on the running of the business and indeed may specify how the business must operate. Contractual obligations included in supplier contracts, aside from stipulating the product to be supplied or service to be performed, may include the provision of timely access to a suitable and safe working environment, transport, special equipment, etc. These more detailed requirements can have a major impact on how the business operates.

c.  Legislation/Regulatory—Ever-changing legislation and regulations can also affect the operation of a business. The ability to translate these into a medium that provides alert management and monitoring can be of great assistance to management by identifying when it is and, more importantly, when it is not meeting requirements. Examples of these organizations/regulations, to name only a few, are U.S. Federal/State/Municipal legislative bodies, The European Union (EU), The Health and Safety Executive (HSE—UK), Sarbanes-Oxley Act, Health Insurance Portability and Accountability Act (HIPAA).

d. Management Requirements—Goals, Plans, Core Values, etc., identified in the initial business plan and generally reviewed on an annual basis. However, without a medium to integrate these requirements into the business they can fall from the forefront of the organization's view. This often happens when the environment becomes intense due to competitive and especially very focused financial pressures. Additionally, deferring the review of management requirements to an annual event makes it difficult to accumulate detail as to why the goals have, or have not, been achieved. Timely and dynamic feedback can assist in measuring progress and facilitating mid-course adjustments to attain the goals.

e. Data—Timely and accurate data is essential to the effective running of the business. In many organizations, the Business Influences provide for rewards or penalties based upon data-related performance. The identification and management of for example contract related data is often essential to compliance and the ongoing profitability, and possibly viability, of the business.

f. Best Practice—When available and substantiated, vertical industry operation (e.g., Manufacturing, Transport, Utilities) and administration (e.g., Finance, HR) best practices such as SCOR, eTOM, etc., are helpful guides to assist in improving the organization's performance. The experiences gained in other vertical industries, especially through the translation of cross-industry semantics, are especially helpful.

This is not an exhaustive list and you may become exhausted just reading it. However, the listing makes the point that a wide variety of Business Influencers and Influences that affect the conduct of the business do exist and that in many cases are very focused. Identification and translation of these Influencers and Influences may be time consuming but the task is necessary and surmountable.

## Business Scenarios

A Business Scenario is a high-level end-to-end business process that produces a revenue product. These scenarios describe the major tasks performed by the business and are created and molded by the Business Influences. By definition, they overlay more than one Business Function, utilizing them to varying degrees, depending upon the functionality required.

One may argue for establishing Business Scenarios before the identification of the Business Influences. The argument could go either way, as the solidification of the Business Influences and Scenarios is an iterative process that eventually settles down as additional detail regarding the management and operation of the business is agreed.

There are two types of Business Scenarios. The first is Business Influence Scenarios. These scenarios translate Influence Requirements to products produced by Influence Management processes. The following is an example of these scenarios:

a. Influence Identification

b. Influence Translation

c. Influence Process/Product Management

The second type is Business Operation Scenarios. There tend to be fewer than five Operation Scenarios upon which a business operates. They are generally unique to the conduct of the business within a vertical industry and the products it delivers. For example, the Facilities Service Management Industry may have three Operations Scenarios. The following is an example of these scenarios:

a. Fault/Incident Rectification

b. Preventive Maintenance

c. Capital Project Management

Business Operation Scenarios usually differ in "complexity" by the amount of time and money that is involved. They tend to vary across vertical industries; however, the fundamental principles are very much the same. The scenario titles should be simple, but meaningful, descriptions of the product produced. In that regard, it is often very difficult for businesses and consultancies who feel that all things are complex to create these statements. The "KISS" principle, Keep It Simple-Stupid, should apply during the creation process. See *Appendix B* for some additional examples.

## Business Function Identification

A Business Function is a high-level group of Influence Management or Operation related organizations that provide a suite of capabilities supporting a certain aspect of the business. The composition of and relationship between Business Functions may vary between industries. However, the business of running the enterprise at Business Function level is surprisingly generic, varying mainly in terms of semantics and nuances from vertical industry to vertical industry. While some may argue this perception, it is common for vertical industries to perceive that their Business Functions are different and complex, citing specific industry semantics to support their argument.

The following are illustrative examples of Influence Management and Operation Functions. See *Appendix E, Semantics* for additional definition.

Influence Management Functions may include:

a. Commercial Management
b. Business Planning
c. Marketing and Communications
d. Health, Safety, Quality & Environment (HSQE)
e. Financial Management
f. Human Resource Management
g. Information Management

Business Operation Functions may include:

a. Macro-Resource Planning
b. Design (Creation)
c. Micro-Resource Planning
d. Delivery

**Function Scenario Creation**

Functions are major components of the Compliance Model and within themselves contain Scenarios which either produce complete internal products, e.g., paid invoice, or components of a final product, e.g., application design. The following are illustrative examples of Influence Management and Operation Function Scenarios:

Influence Management identifies business applicable requirements from influencers and translates them into the required products and supporting processes needed to deliver them.

a. Commercial Management—Tender Management, Procurement, Contract Administration

b. Business Planning—Manage Strategy, Acquire Capital, Manage Investment

c. Marketing—Manage Opportunities, Manage Accounts, Manage Promotions

d. Health—Manage Stress & Fatigue, Manage Drugs & Alcohol, Manage Flexible Working

e. Safety—Manage Assurance, Manage System Risk, Manage Risk Contribution

f. Quality—Manage Supplier Base, Manage Service Quality, Manage Product Quality

g. Environment—Manage Environmental Aspects, Manage Hazardous Material, Manage Waste

h. Financial Management—Manage Receivables, Manage Payables, Manage Treasury

i. Human Resource Management—Recruit to Hire, Manage Employee Life Cycle, Manage Competence

j. Information Technology Management—Manage Assets, Manage Service, Manage Security

Operation Management receives Business Influence translation requirements in the form of processes and required products and applies them to the creation and delivery of revenue generating products.

a. Macro Resource Planning Management: Product Delivery Planning, Operation Resource Planning, Work Package/Project Creation

b. Design (Creation) Management: Project (Activity/Task) Plan Definition, Planned Work Package Creation

c. Micro-Resource Planning Management: Detailed Work Planning, Release of Fully Qualified Work Packages

d. Delivery Management: Work Management, Work Commissioning, Handover and Acceptance Management

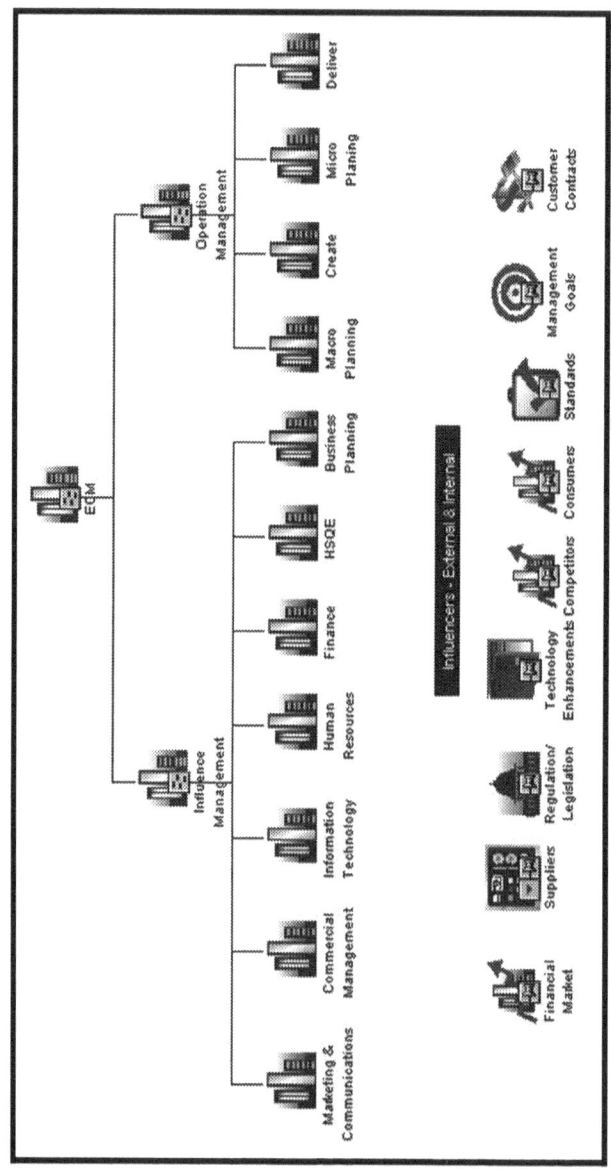

*Figure 4—Organization Model Example*

## The Organization Model

The model of the organization (*See Figure 4, Organization Model*) created to support the Compliance Model environment focuses on the roles, teams, and groups utilized by the scenarios and processes. In that regard, the model is not a detailed organization chart but a functional structure that may initially reflect traditional organizational groupings. The latter tends to be particularly true for the Influence Management function.

The creation and population of the planned organization or "To-Be" model, based upon the Compliance Model structure, is very helpful during the Manage Processes phase of the *Create the Compliance Environment* section of this Guide.

The current or "As-Is" organization should also be created to establish the baseline from which change will take place. This organization will evolve to the planned "To-Be" organization during the implementation of ECM and sometimes beyond.

It is very helpful to have these organizations, especially the "To-Be" organization, on a single sheet of paper, webpage, or other medium available to members of the business for easy reference.

## Elemental Information

We have grouped Elemental information, for purposes of this discussion, into three areas: Data, Content, and Applications. These are important because they act as accumulators during Influence Identification & Translation.

1   Data—Business Influences, especially contracts, may contain clauses for failure to perform. More often than not, there are a number of quantifiable clauses which could have significant impact on the business should performance not be as agreed. If one researches these one usually finds that the information required is a small set of data, which, if properly managed, would minimize the occurrences of noncompliance.

There is another important use for data and that is the identification of attributes maintained throughout the system for cataloguing, searching, and reporting. Group these attributes under headings such as Work Breakdown Structure, Cost, Location, Abbreviations, Content Management, Applications, etc. Experience has shown, however, that attributes and their associated abbreviations are generally the most difficult to agree on and keep simple. One rule of thumb is that a combination of no more than six attributes should be required to obtain a reasonable sample of the data or information required.

2   Content—In many businesses, content tends to be mismanaged. This is frequently an understatement. A significant cause of the problem is the lack of understanding of what comprises the structure of a message and its importance to the business. The ability to manage messages and therefore content plays an important part in the creation of processes and products and the success of ECM.

I have seen many businesses become bogged down in attempting to implement a content management system to "get rid of the paper" as opposed to utilizing it as one of the tools to help address process optimization and compliance. Curb the tendency for a quick hit and stick to the Guide unless cleaning off all the desks is the only purpose for the initiative. If the latter is the case, then the paper will soon reappear.

One technique to reduce paper that I have seen work effectively is the requirement for the company president to sign all requisitions for cabinets, boxes and folders used for filing. Attention soon focuses on the root cause of the paper and ways of amending processes to remove its existence.

3   Applications—One of the expected results of an ECM implementation is the reduction in the number of disparate IT software applications, and their associated repositories utilized to operate the business. It is important to note that in this top-down approach the focus should be on the Business Influences, Scenarios, and Processes, and the needs thereof. Taking the "what we have is good enough" view of some IT—rather than business oriented—professionals without first establishing and applying the ECM top-down optimization will only perpetuate existing inefficiencies and non value added costs.

Note that in today's world many IT managers and staff have not had business training and as a result will provide solutions from a technical rather than a business standpoint. Many times their research yields common solutions in the industry based upon the latest technology, "best of breed", etc., when in fact you may need something altogether different. Keep close to the Guide and stick to your requirements and you will find your solution. In all the years' I have been implementing systems I have never been held back by technology; although sometimes application solutions, once identified, have taken a while to get through IT.

As with data, the effort here should be to identify the core applications currently operating within the business, as well as any new applications planned for implementation. Then match the applications capabilities against the Business Influence, Scenario & Process requirements and address the resulting gaps with value added (that does not necessarily equate to high cost) expenditures.

# The Compliance Environment

## Overview

The Compliance Environment utilizes the Reference & Infrastructure Environments and the Compliance Model together with the Influence Management and Operation Scenarios and their processes and products to establish the structure for managing compliance.

## The Compliance Model

The creation of a Compliance Model, a high-level graphical representation depicting the relationship between each of the components that influence and manage the business enterprise, is essential. The model helps to relate the concept of the business to its employees and to its world. The model may also benefit the sales and/or purchase negotiation process to relate compliance commitment to customers and/or suppliers.

The optimum portrayal of the model is on a single sheet of paper or webpage, made available throughout the organization as a reminder of management's focus on compliance. It consists of four domains: Customer Influences, Supplier Influences, Competitor Influences, and the Compliance Domain. It is of note that customers, suppliers, and competitors may be internal or external to the organization.

The Compliance Model shown in *Figure 1* is an example of one created from information gathered while working in a number of vertical industries. This model is utilized throughout this guide as the baseline example for the creation of the business specific model described in the following *Create the Compliance Environment* section.

## Business Influence Scenarios

### Influence Identification

As stated previously, influences are the reasons for being in business and may greatly affect the way a business operates. One should not attempt the prioritization of translation without first assuring the identification of all of the influences that will possibly affect the business.

However, identification is an evolution, not just a one-off exercise. A business will add, change, or remove influences on an ongoing basis. Therefore, administrative processes and products must be in place to manage this ever-changing environment.

## Influence Translation

Influence Translation is sometimes very difficult. However, it is the most important task of the organization managing the business. Influence Translation provides for the sustainability of the business through the creation of validated business requirements in the form of products supplied by Influence Management or Operations. Translation generally includes the following elements:

a. Quantification—Identify and quantify compliance indices, service levels, deliverables, goals, KPIs, etc., in order to establish the desired level of performance. Translation that is not specific leads to further ambiguity and almost certainly failure to meet expected or perceived performance levels. I have been involved in post contract signing discussions where the customer expected that our organization would fail to quantify influences and that our performance would therefore be subject to attribution. That was not a pleasant thought as we were in start-up mode. We quickly addressed the situation and removed the perception.

b. Responsibility—Identifying the owner of the Business Influence, and the owner's role such as internal, customer, supplier, and third party provider, is necessary in establishing the definitive source for Business Influence definition, clarity, composition, and requirements.

c. Timing—The type of Influence will most likely dictate timing. Influence requirements may be one-off or repetitive activities occurring on a pre-determined or ad-hoc basis. There should be no surprise requirements.

d. Influence Relationships—Few Influences are independent of one another. In fact, many have overlapping requirements and/or priorities. In that respect, one must carefully manage relationships in order to reduce any misalignment of priorities and information between functions and the resulting counter productive effort that could easily be detrimental to the business as a whole. I have seen, for example, P&L meetings where marketing, planning, finance, manufacturing and procurement were all providing different results numbers based upon their view of the pervious period. A year later and after applying the ECM concept, the company was running error-minimized trial balances on a weekly basis, a clear indication of influence alignment.

e. Data—Data is the lowest form of information in business and underpins everything it does. Interestingly enough, in the business of running the business there is a fundamental set of data that must adhere to standards

(See illustrative examples in *Appendix C, Elemental Standards*) for the business to operate. Added to that is the data that applies to the specific operation of the business.

For example, contracts usually contain penalty clauses for failure to perform. There are, more often than not, a small number of clauses that can significantly affect the business for not achieving performance as agreed. Careful examination of the contractual clauses usually reveals a manageable set of data that, if adequately monitored, can alleviate a significant amount of distress. The management of processes affecting this data minimizes and assists in making the occurrences of the failure attributable. Note that it is not the data that minimizes attribution, but its management. It is important to insure that you address data consistently along the entire Information Supply Chain, passing the same requirements for accurate data through to suppliers providing services that meet your contractual requirements.

f. Organization—Roles identify responsibility within scenarios/processes. In order to understand the impact of a role, it is important to relate it to the proposed organization. This provides an understanding of the relationships between responsible roles and assists in their management during the evolution of the organization.

### Influence Process/Product Management

The output of Influence Translation is formed into a suite of products and supporting processes that become a part of the Influence Management and Operation functions. The implementation of these products and processes occurs on an as-needed basis in support of Influence Requirements.

## The Infrastructure Environment

### Overview

The design of the Infrastructure Environment must provide for a dynamic and responsive setting to support the Reference and Compliance Environment. This is accomplished by providing comprehensive and integrated application software capability with which to store and maintain the reference information across a flexible and secure network.

### Application Software

The minimum capabilities required in the selection of an application software suite are as follows:

a. Repositories to store or link to the information gathered or identified.

b. Organizational Model to map and manage current (As-is) organizational roles as well as those proposed for (To-be) changes.

c. Portals for accumulating and providing access to customer information.

d. Process Management providing the capability to manage the library of business scenarios/processes and support information gathering.

e. Process Automation to provide collaborative scenario and process prototyping utilizing a process automation engine and simulation tools.

The provision of an inter-operable product suite is paramount for the efficient accumulation and management, and effective dissemination, of reference information through portals, web pages, etc.

Review products in the marketplace to ascertain which offerings are very close to providing a complete package. Consider these prior to attempting the creation of a bespoke environment or relying on a cheap and cheerful alternative. The latter alternative, in the end, is generally more costly to maintain and frequently does not provide the robustness necessary for the ultimate consumer's ease of access.

It is important to focus on your requirements and how the application software addresses them rather than rely in the 'requirements' provided by the software vendor or a consultancy firm, both of which are focused on selling their wares, generally under the guise of "best practice".

## Communications Network

The requirement for robust network infrastructure is equally important to the continuing success of ECM. There will be a considerable investment in effort and knowledge if one follows the ECM Guide. Constructing the model on a less than adequate network is tempting disaster. The consumer may find it difficult to obtain information if the response is slow or the system or network crashes on a regular basis. In addition, the information gathered forms the fundamental knowledge upon which the organization depends and operates. The loss of that knowledge, and/or the inability to keep it up to date, will nullify the time and effort invested in the Guide and potentially put the organization at risk.

# Create the Compliance Environment

The following sequence of activities (*See Figure 5—Steps to Compliance*) addresses techniques that assist in as streamlined an implementation of ECM as possible. Effectively applied, the techniques provide guidance to address challenges that may otherwise hinder progress.

# Preparation

Preparation facilitates success. It should comprise most of the effort expended to initiate an ECM environment within an enterprise. The project is at risk and should not be initiated if the management of the implementation team is unwilling to spend time and resources on preparation.

# Create the Management Environment

The organization must be committed to proceed with the implementation of the ECM environment. Without total commitment, ECM will fail to produce the desired operational optimization and will have caused disruption in the conduct of the business

Managing the environment is essential to success of the endeavor. The highest-level management support ensures that the people and processes are in place to manage creation and change. The following, therefore, are major contributors that must be in place to ensure success:

### Sponsor Support

The main sponsor should be an executive member of the board. The sponsor must not only understand ECM at a high level but also be able to market the concepts well enough to convince the unconvinced, bringing them into the fold. The main sponsor's effort starts with selling the initial concept to the board and continues by providing ongoing support thereafter. The sponsor's ability to maintain momentum will ensure the success of ECM and the organization's goals. Without the main board's buy-in and the sponsor's involvement, the initiative is inherently at risk.

I choose the most powerful and persuasive member of the board to sponsor the initiative and to ensure the continuation of the ECM environment. That individual's task is to assure board management understanding, involvement, and support. These are essential for the success of ECM as well as other projects that have a significant impact on the business.

### Stakeholder Involvement

The sponsor cannot act alone. He or she requires full support from the business community. That support must come from the key stakeholders, the management owners of the Business, and Function Scenarios. They form part of the core Implementation Management Team and are responsible for the successful implementation of the ECM environment.

Initially, there may be difficulty identifying the stakeholders until agreement of the Influencers and Scenarios. If that is the case, and the sponsor is unsure, then he or she should appoint those whom he or she thinks would most likely be the stakeholders with the caveat that the composition of the team may change as the implementation progresses.

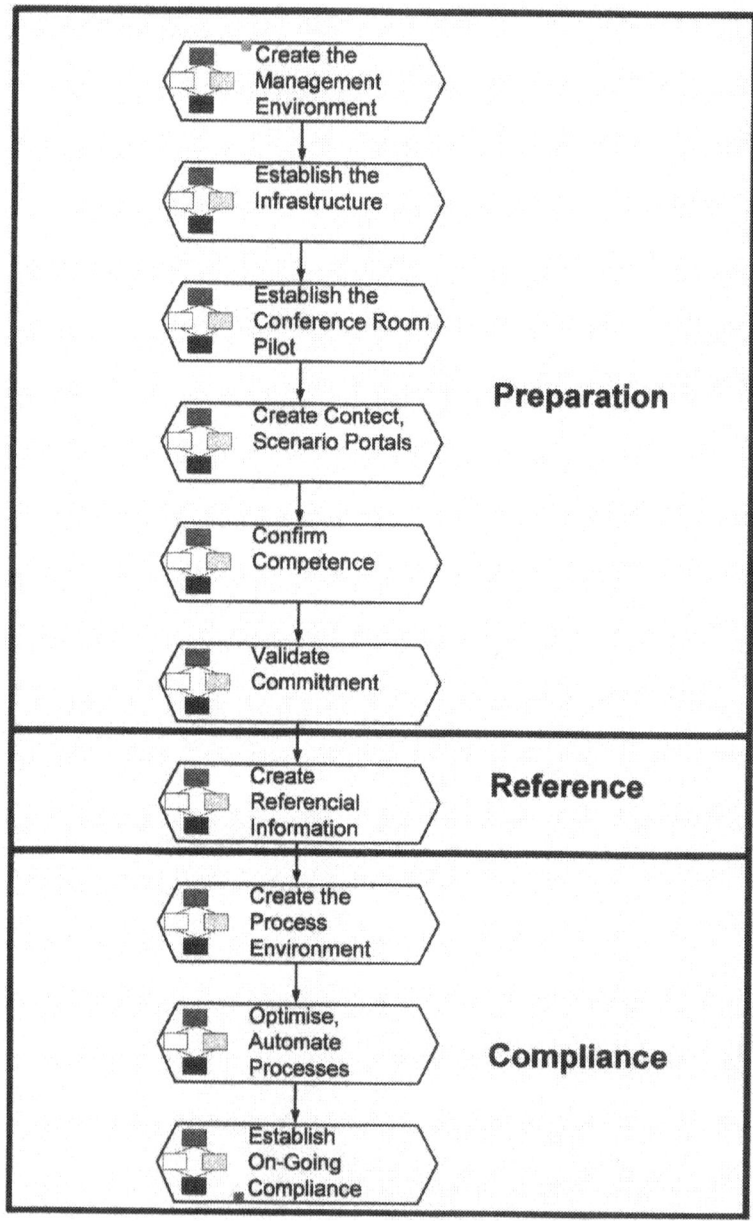

*Figure 5—Steps to Compliance*

## Process Coordinator Inclusion

Once the sponsor and stakeholders are established, the identification of the Process Coordinators should follow. The identification and inclusion of the Process Coordinators is of particular importance because they are essential to providing practical business expertise and the necessary day-to-day implementation support. The Process Coordinators must be involved practitioners from the business functions and provide the focal point for process management activities. I have found that these individuals already exist in the functional areas and are easily identified. They are generally the recognized font of local knowledge.

ECM competence validation with supporting training and recognition ensure that the Process Coordinators are ready to accept their challenge. Management must be at their side to help them from the outset of the implementation, as it may seem that their job effort may be significantly increased. Where necessary, the coordinators should be provided additional resource to get over the initial effort required. In the medium to long term, however, the benefits of the ECM implementation will kick in and will help to simplify their efforts and reduce their load.

I was involved in one implementation that began with the Process Coordinators (we called the Module Administrators) working ten hours a day, six days a week. In less than six months they were working six hours a day, five days a week and spending the other two hours trying to make the environment even better; an incremental increase in their quality of life.

Management should make ECM a part of the everyday fabric of the business without the addition of either permanent staff or ongoing consultancy. Almost certainly, one can utilize employees already on the payroll to make ECM a success. They are the business's real power. Harness their energy and talents, help them with competence based training, and they will help you attain a Continuing Compliance environment.

## Ongoing Implementation Team

The Sponsor and Process Coordinators require support from the business community. Ensure that those involved come from the business. They have the knowledge and equally (if not more) important, they have a stake in gaining improvements.

## Create & Validate Standards

Time spent establishing standards at the beginning of the implementation will pay back immeasurably as it progresses. As a minimum, establish standards for the creation and management of the following:

a. The Compliance Model and its components;

b. Influence Identification, Translation, and Process/Product Creation;

c. Organizational Model;

d. Elemental Information;

e. Infrastructure Applications;

f. The Solution Center;

g. Portals;

h. Competence; and,

i. The Process Environment.

Even though these standards will inevitably evolve as the implementation progresses, it is important to have an established standards as a starting point and recognition that once the evolution has started they must be successfully managed.

## Establish the Infrastructure

Some of the most well intentioned implementations fall seriously short of the mark when the infrastructure lacks the required capabilities to support them. The shortcomings may range from major holes in the applications to the inability of the consumer to input or access his or her required information.

The infrastructure environment contains the repositories that hold the Reference information as well as providing the facilities for the Business Process Library, Portals, and Process Automation. See *Figure 3, Structure Overview* for a conceptual overview of this environment.

It is important to the success of ECM to have an infrastructure wherein each of the components seamlessly inter-operates with all others.

### Identify the Application Software Suite

There is no one software application that supports the total ECM concept; at least I have not found one. The market does however provide a number of applications that address a variety of capabilities. See *Appendix D, Information Providers* for an illustrative list of professional organizations' websites where one may find listings of available products. As a whole, these offerings possess the capabilities necessary to address the needs of ECM. Carefully choose a suite of integrate-able products that provide capabilities in the following four areas:

1. The Compliance Environment—Most probably, there are products in the marketplace that address the Compliance and Organization Models, Scenarios, Portals, Data, Content, Application and Process Libraries, and Work Flow as an integrated suite of capabilities. One should consider products like these before launching into an extensive search for, and integration of, individual point solution—sometimes-called "best of breed"—products. The latter often cause increases in effort, opportunity cost, and delay.

   A comment concerning workflow is appropriate here. Workflow, currently evolving to Business Process Management (BPM), can be an extremely powerful process automation enabler. Workflow is fast becoming a part of many application solution products and each supplier claims it is a facilitator of the ultimate solution. Take care to insure that the individual product workflow capabilities do not foster separate workflow camps within the business and IT. One way to combat this situation is to determine at the outset which workflow/BPM tool will be the core that either replaces all others or draws all others to it for integration. To that end, a separate, robust Business Process Management package may be required to be the engine that integrates into all the other software application products.

   Specific capabilities that require identification are:

   a. The Compliance Model—The ability to automatically create and manage the evolution of the Model in graphical terms on a single sheet of paper, or webpage, is helpful in marketing the concept. This high-level representation provides a concise picture for all of the major Business Influences. *See Figure 1, Compliance Model* for an example of the model.

   b. Business Scenarios—Provide the ability to create and manage the high level, end-to-end processes that create the products provided by the business. See an example of a Business Operation Scenario, Fault/Incident Reporting in *Figure 6.*

c.  The Business Influences—Business Influences are the reasons for being in business and the factors by which they are constrained. Examples of influences are Contracts, Regulations, Standards, Legislation, and Management Goals. *Figure 7, Business Influence Standard* provides and example of the next level of detail for the EFQM Business Influence Standard. At the highest level, these are displayed on the Compliance Model. Their components provide input to the creation and maintenance of the Scenarios, Processes and Products established to support compliance.

d.  Portals—Portals facilitate the structure of the consumer-contextual-knowledge-repository views required by departments, teams, etc. *Figure 8* shows an example of a contextual Portal for Human Resources. The ability for the consumer to manage these on an ongoing basis is important to their effective utilization.

e.  The Organizational Model—Provide the ability to create a succession of Organizational Models linked with the elements of the Compliance Model to track relationships and the effects of the migration of compliance and its processes and products. See *Figure 4* for an example of an ECM oriented Organization.

f.  The Data/Content/Application Library—Provide the ability to create and manage a repository for Data, Content, and Application definitions and related links.

g.  The Business Process Library—Establish a structured environment for the storage and management of business scenarios and processes.

h.  Process Automation—As processes become refined, and may benefit from automation, they are converted utilizing consumer oriented Workflow. The statistical information gained through prudent use of Workflow capabilities can provide important dynamic feedback which, if properly implemented, improves the effectiveness of the scenarios and processes.

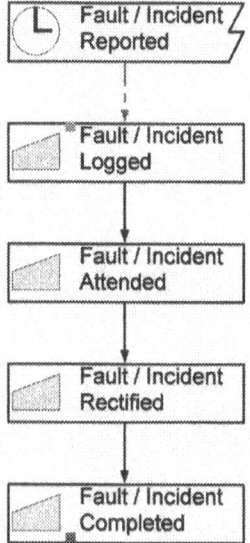

*Figure 6—Business Operation Scenario Example*
Fault/Incident Reporting

2. Content Management—The creation of the Reference Environment will most likely result in the conversion of some of the Business Influences, which are generally in disparate electronic or paper form, into the reference medium. In that regard, the requirement for content management application software may be reduced somewhat. However, the capability is still necessary for a variety of other requirements, e.g., where there is a need to have an electronic copy of an original document, such as a signed contract. As time passes, additional documentation may need to be stored to support changes.

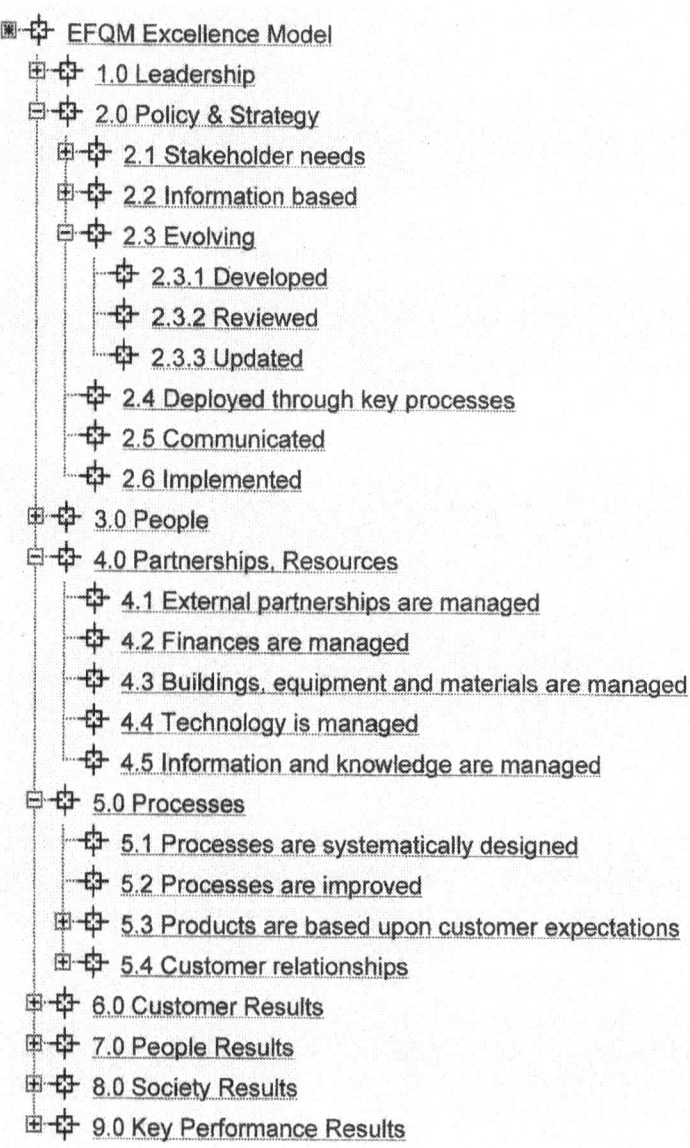

*Figure 7—EFQM—Business Influence Standard Example*

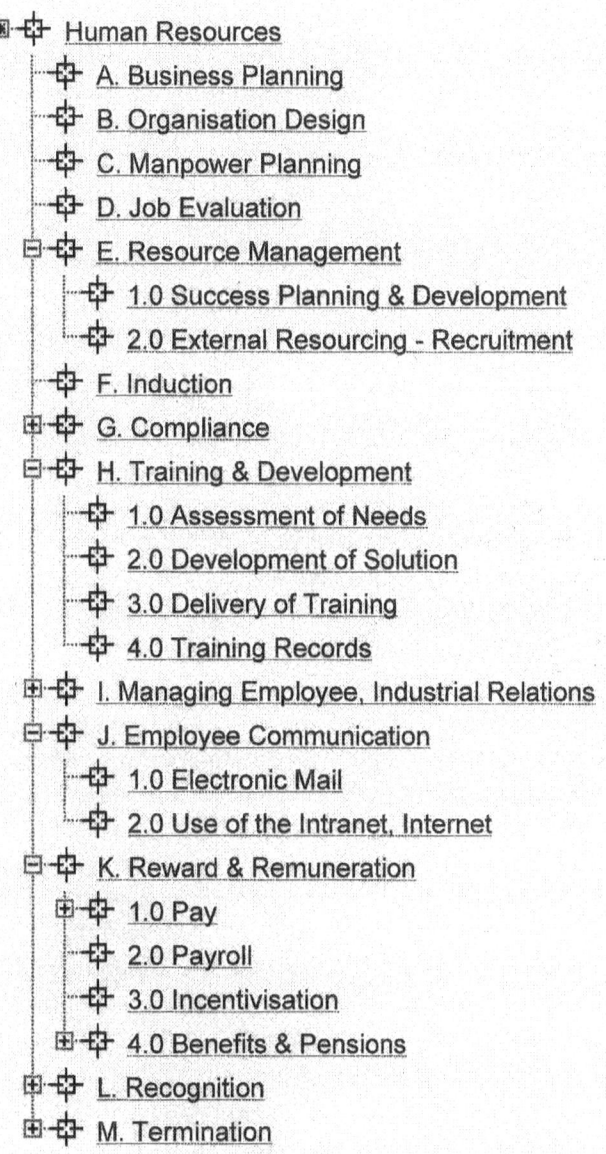

*Figure 8—Human Resources Context Portal Example*

The Content Management solution may be as simple as a file management system on a PC or the implementation of a robust Content Management tool. In most businesses, a content (document) management tool already exists in some form or other. Therefore, the identification of, and integration with, a Content Management tool is extremely helpful during the initial population of the Reference Environment.

There are a significant number of Content Management packages in the marketplace. Overall, their capabilities are very competitive, although some have additional niche specialization. See *Appendix D, Information Providers* for more information.

Take care during the selection and implementation of a Content Management application to ensure that the implementation team remains focused on the task: the implementation of ECM. The primary aim is to optimize requirements messages and in so doing reduce the amount of paper and electronic media that plagues the organization. Content Management is part of the facilitating infrastructure. Therefore, it should not be a separate initiative aimed at converting all the business paperwork into digital form just to clean off the desks and reduce the number of filing cabinets. The paper will return without the inclusion of process optimization.

3. Office Automation—Office Automation suites are extensively used in most organizations. However, there is nothing more frustrating for a consumer than to try to update or view a document when the necessary tools are neither at their disposal nor compatible. It is important to ensure that these products are available, compatible, and integrated with other components of the ECM suite. Application compatibility helps to increase productivity while decreasing effort, frustration and therefore cost within an organization. If you do not believe this then try operating your finance department utilizing five different revision levels of Excel. I know one company that tried because it was too "expensive" to bring everyone up to the same version.

4. Communication—Communication constitutes more than the cables and a robust LAN/WAN. It is a fundamental enabler for the consumer, in an environment regulated by applicable security measures, to access information freely and easily. This Customer Relationship Management aspect of your Information Technology Services organization must constantly monitor this environment to ensure comprehensive consumer access. I know "security" is an issue, it always is. However, it is more important to provide power to the consumer than to keep capabilities locked up and "safeguarded" by IT. Too often, I have seen "security" used as an excuse not to provide a capability because of the effort involved.

# Establish a Solution Center Environment

A Solution Center (sometimes called a Conference Room Pilot) is the equivalent of a live operational environment, but in a test mode. Its purpose is to provide a physical and/or virtual collaborative location, often called a "War Room," where implementation trials can take place. Many of today's content management application solutions, to assist in facilitating the Solution Center, offer online collaboration. This feature provides an environment where a number of individuals may interact across the network in a virtual manner, resulting in the following positive benefits:

a. Team members may attend virtual meetings at a moment's notice to address situations requiring immediate attention. Virtual collaboration may therefore preclude the need for a physical "War Room." The addition of Video Conferencing, if available, further enhances dialogue, increases inclusion and helps to flush out hidden agendas that may hinder progress. I have found that because of time zone restrictions which occur during video conferencing sessions attendees tend to arrive on time, are better prepared and are more attentive.

b. Team members should be able to operate from their desks, or other desks as appropriate, to join in discussions, thus reducing travel related delay and its associated non-productive time.

c. All discussions, markups, and conclusions are generally documented as part of the collaboration so there should be no delay in "getting the minutes out," thus reducing the subsequent concern that the information provided was not complete, accurate or agreed.

However, make every effort to insure that the team members meet face-to-face on a regular basis. Time for socializing should be a major part of these meetings, providing a platform for synergistic discussions. Making provision for a team member to describe verbally a success experienced in one part of the implementation often provides a catalyst for further discussions in another. Without these meetings, the tendency for the team members is to become increasingly isolated and return to their daily tasks.

Solution Centers have proven to be extremely effective in reducing delivery time, minimizing cost, and increasing implementation success. Solution Centers provide a medium facilitating:

a. the validation of the chosen application suite of software and implementation concepts against the requirements of Business Influence, Scenarios, and Processes;

b. the establishment of standards as quality validation points for review and confirmation;

c. concept testing of new process concepts, application software upgrades, etc., without affecting the production environment;

d. assessment of the appropriate use of management and delivery media;

e. the marketing of ECM concepts to the disbelievers and validation to those who believe.

## Create Portals

Portals are windows into the information contained in the Reference and Process Repositories. Portals may be consumer contextual, i.e., created for the specific needs of the consumer, or Business/Function Scenario oriented views.

Portals may be utilized to translate Business Influence textual information such as Standards, Regulations, Contracts, etc., into a medium (See *Figure 7, Business Influence Standard Example*) that provides easy access as well as contextual links to supporting websites, processes, procedures, etc. A controlled environment, due to the nature of the content, ensures that Business Influence text information remains current and applicable. This is the first step in reducing paperwork within ECM.

One of the possible benefits of a Portal is its ability to allow the ultimate consumer to create a personalized, functional, or departmental view of the information in the repository. These views may evolve as the needs of the consumer change. Placing the management of Portals in the hands of the consumer reduces the frustration and effort associated with inability or delay in attempting to obtain information. Your IT department may disapprove of its "lack of control" by placing power in the hands of the consumer. If the transition is not structured properly then they are right. However, I can tell you from experience that when the transition is structured properly, the payback is substantial.

The application software suite should provide consumer-oriented capabilities with which to establish and change views as their needs evolve. These capabilities should reduce the frustration associated with waiting for, for example, an Information Technology specialist to accomplish the task for them. The following examples provided some illustrations:

a. Business Influences—Note that in the Business Influence Standards example (*See Fig. 7*) the translation of the standard text is to high-level requirements topics. Although not shown in the example, the software suite should provide the capability of adding links to each of the topic headings. These links, generally required to establish compliance, may be to processes, documentation, or websites providing for a hierarchy of governance environment.

b. Compliance Model—Compliance models vary from business to business. See *Figure 1* for a common representation. The suite should have the capability to create a Compliance Model as the top level of the hierarchy of Scenarios, Processes and Products. Once created, dynamic linking between levels should identify report any anomalies.

c. Business and Function Scenarios—Scenarios are high-level end-to-end processes within the business. See *Figure 8* for an example of a portal created for the Function Scenario/Human Resources Life-Cycle. Business and Function Scenarios should be created and maintained by Process Management.

d. Organization Model—Organizations may change as the Compliance Environment evolves, adding, changing, or deleting new roles, teams, or even groups. Having the capability to relate the organization structure to the roles and functions identified (*See Figure 4*) through the compliance process becomes a powerful tool in analyzing the effects of the evolution.

e. Elemental Library—The Elemental Library is a repository for commonly used data elements within ECM. The software's capability should provide for consistency in definition across the model, i.e., one version of the truth.

## Confirm Competence

It is one thing to have tools and another to utilize them effectively. At this point in the Guide, our concentration should be on the execution of activities and the effective utilization of the products provided to attain compliance. That is why competence is so important. Competence is more than just training. It is a reliable way of monitoring occupational skills and underpinning knowledge.

People generally perform better if they know clearly and precisely what they should be doing to be effective at their jobs. Vital to this is a clear statement of the skills, knowledge, and attributes needed to be successful. The generic term for these statements and an individual's ability to attain the outcomes that they seek is "competence."

There is a general sequence of activities geared toward attaining competence. Different organizations are able to adapt them easily to match their exact needs. In that regard, competence can be a valuable strategic weapon for increasing business or a tool for identifying training needs. It all depends on how far each individual organization is willing to use its power.

Validate that the environment and its participants are prepared to move forward to ensure success. Accomplish this through the following:

1 Standards Creation—Creation of implementation standards for information format, input, display, and maintenance is especially important when dealing with Elemental information such as Content, Data, and Applications. See *Appendix C* for a list of examples.

2 Assessment Creation—Competence assessment templates used for assessing team members as well as providing them with the tools required to work with key members of their organizations.

3 Assessment Application—Conduct assessments to ascertain the level of knowledge within the organization. It should be no surprise if the results of the assessments show a high level of existing staff competence.

4 Identify Training Needs—Utilize assessments to identify training needs.

5 Create Training & Involvement Programs—Create training programs to ensure those with demonstrated needs have been addressed. The common technique of sending everyone through all the training courses without assessments to "ensure they have been trained" is expensive, delays the program, and does not necessarily ensure competence.

6 Conduct Training & Involvement Programs—It is rare for any initiative to succeed without the involvement of the ultimate consumer. This, integrated with training, provides the ultimate marketing and implementation tool.

7 Validate Competence—Validating competence through testing proves the successful application of the program.

8 Acknowledge Success—More than anything else, *acknowledge the success of those involved.*

Everyone can benefit from the use of a competence program. Training needs will automatically become easier to identify and prioritize. Training will become more effective because the competence statements will sharpen the focus and set the standard. As a result, those people employed by an organization that uses a competence program will benefit as a team and make a more consistent contribution to the overall success of the business. Competence will also greatly improve selection and recruitment, consistent job descriptions, performance appraisal, career planning and promotion.

## Validate On-going Commitment

At this point is important to undertake a review of the status of each of the tasks attempted so far. They should all be complete and to the satisfaction of the Implementation Team, who must express a solid commitment to proceed. Address any question of concern and agree upon a course of action prior to moving forward. The next suite of tasks will probably be more frustrating than difficult and the team will welcome the removal of any issue or obstacle that will hinder their future progress.

## Create Reference Information

Having established the implementation team, ensured their competence, and implemented the infrastructure to facilitate the accumulation of information, initiate the following sequence of events to establish the Reference Environment upon which ECM will rely:

1. Identify Business Influences—The identification of all Business Influences is essential. Accomplish this with an Implementation Team brainstorming session. However, validate the results through interview sessions with senior management and key members of the Influence Management staff. There is a good possibility that the discussions may raise inquiries for further research. These must be resolved to ensure that the identification has been as exhaustive as possible.

   Once a set of Influences is agreed, the next task is to understand their interrelationships and prioritize their translation. Understanding their interrelationships is most important because various influences affecting the same function may have differing goals. For example, a Finance goal may be to drive inventory to "zero", while Marketing's goal may require additional inventory "Just in Case" there is a sale. Operations on the other hand may want a "Just in Time" inventory environment. Examples like these more often than not drive differing inventory expectations within the company. All of the inventory influences must be reconciled prior to translating the requirements to processes and the products expected from the business. Obviously, the administrative process-es for managing this environment must be in place to assure the ongo-ing validation of the current influences and the inclusion of new ones as they become apparent.

The infrastructure should facilitate documenting any applicable ref-erences found during the identification of the Business Influences and as the opportunities arise in the Elemental Data repository. These will most likely be helpful when documenting Influence Translations. In addition, the infrastructure should facilitate the accumulation and translation of Business Influences into an easily accessible form. Their content may be translated into the ECM application solution suite, or they may be linked to the original text stored in a Content Management system, website, or specific bookmark on a website.

2. Translate Business Influences—Translating the Business Influences into the scenarios and processes to which the business must comply and products that it must produce is not as easy as it may seem. The follow-ing sequence may be helpful to the translation process:

a) Applicability Level—Determine, in general, the influence's applica-bility to the business. For example, all of ISO:9001 may be applicable to a business, but only part of ISO:14000.

b) Conversion—Many influences have a table of contents or a high-level hierarchy of topics. Convert these into a portal (*See Figure 7, Business Influence Example*). It is helpful to include the text associat-ed with each of the topics for further reference. One of the outputs of the Influence Translation exercise should be the identification of core data. As stated earlier, this data is generally critical to the ethical, as well as commercial, interests of the organization.

c) Requirement Identification/Linking—During the conversion from the requirements native media to a portal, identify and highlight requirements messages. This forms the basis for linking the message requirement from the portal both up to the source of the require-ment and down to the internal documents and supporting manage-ment, e.g., add, change, and delete processes. Another output of the identification of specific requirements is the identification of oppor-tunities for improvement resulting from the translation of Business Influences. The opportunities include references that may be incor-rect or missing; and/or documentation that may be incomplete or out of date. Some of these opportunities become immediately obvious while others surface during the Process Creation phase of this Guide's implementation.

d) Compliance Product Creation—The most effective way to communicate compliance is to have processes in place that provide the knowledge that the intended receiver of a requirement message has received it, read it, understood it, and acted appropriately. This is the essence of requirements message compliance.

3. Create the Business Scenarios—A Business Scenario is a high-level end-to-end Business Influence or Operation Management process that overlays more than one Business Function. From a purist standpoint, one would start with the creation of the Influence Management Scenarios because they define the compliance products required from the business.

4. Identify the Business Functions—A Business Function (*See Appendix B, Business Function/Scenario Example*) is a high-level group of Influence or Operation Management related functions that provide a suite of capabilities as well as internal products supporting a particular aspect of the business. Many of the Influence Management Functions are traditional, e.g., HR, Finance, IT, Business Planning and the like. The Operation Management Functions are generally specific to the vertical industry, e.g., Manufacturing, Banking, Insurance, etc.

5. Identify the Function Scenarios—A Function Scenario is a high-level end-to-end process that occurs within a Function. Here again, many of the Influence Management Functional Scenarios are traditional. The Operation Management Functional Scenarios tend to be unique to the nature of the business.

6. Create the Organizational Model—Once the Business Model and Scenarios have been created, it is time to establish the "As-Is" Organizational Model. The "To-Be" Organizational Model should then be created as far as it may be understood. A major part of this exercise is establishing and defining the roles, teams, and groups in the Elemental Data repository. The high-level roles, as a minimum, will be required when assigning the scenario process owners.

7. Identify Elemental Information—It is important that the team accumulate elemental information as it becomes available while focusing on that which is of primarily importance to the Guide, i.e., Business Influence Translation. The core elemental data repository includes:

a) Data—Generally, there is a small group of data important to the successful operation of the business, accumulated in the elemental repository and managed according to established standards.

b) Content—Content requirements vary from business to business. However, the need for standards addressing the attributes applied to content and their maintenance is of paramount importance. Without the application of attribute standards, content easily accumulates in an unstructured manner, making it difficult to manage and retrieve.

c) Application Systems—Identification of the business system applications currently employed by the business as well as those in the implementation plan is an important but sometimes difficult task. Creation of an initial inventory of these applications prior to embarking on the *Create the Process Environment* phase of the Guide will establish a starting point for the accumulation and use of application information going forward.

## Create the Process Environment

Once the Function Scenarios are established, the team should link existing processes and add or correct missing or incomplete processes.

Business Influence translation may result in varying emphases and priorities placed on Influence Management and Operation Scenarios. The effect of this translation eventually ripples through to the processes and the products that support them. The result of these effects may vary greatly between the Influence Management and Operation Management and require the need for process and product information feedback and reconciliation capability to assure compliance and identify current or potential opportunities.

The situation becomes more complicated when there is a variety of systems information to integrate. Employ the capabilities of a Business Process Management system when, due to the number of variables that require addressing, the need is extensive or complex.

The identification of current or potential opportunities during the management of the process and product reconciliation requires a robust administrative process that in itself feeds the opportunity information back to the Business Influences (*See Figure 2, Influence Management Process Overview*) for further consideration. The correction of some opportunities may seem to be advantageous at a downstream process level. However, raising their profile by addressing them at the Business Influence level helps to assure that their implementation is consistent with the direction of the business as a whole.

Sometimes the visibility raises additional opportunities for improvement that lower level processes may not consider. I have seen, more times than I would like to remember, a low-level initiative by an aspiring clerk to cut off payments to suppliers who have not conformed to a specific payment format procedure in Accounts Payable. This resulted in components required for shipments being placed on hold, halting production and therefore shipments and revenue. Suddenly working to rule without rationalizing its effect on the rest of the business can easily put it at risk.

It is important to note, if one adheres to the ECM Guide's sequence of implementation, that a significant amount of work has to take place before the creation and initiation of the Process Environment phase. Many initiatives start with low-level processes, focusing on statistical specifics without having the benefit of being put into perspective within the total scheme of the business. In that respect, their singularly focused optimization may be inconsistent with other individual process-optimization initiatives or the required direction of the business, and as a result cause more harm than good, or no good at all.

Processes, with their allied work instructions, direct the operation of the organization. Creation of a robust process repository is therefore important to the success of the environment. See an example of a business Capital Project Management Process in *Figure 9*.

Creation of the Process Environment consists of the following activities:

1. Create the Topic Hierarchy—Create a high-level topic hierarchy including each of the previously identified Business Scenarios and Functions from the Business Model. The Topic Hierarchy is a way of organizing your information by establishing a framework for the Reference Repository. The hierarchy facilitates links to Influences, Scenarios, Functions, Elemental Information, and Processes. *Figure 10* illustrates a Topic Hierarchy of a Facilities or Service Management organization. Note that this structure will evolve with the addition of each new topic and that this, like the other portals, is another example of a window into the Reference repository.

2. Create Organization and Elemental Data—Upon establishing the Topic Hierarchy one can add or link, as appropriate, Roles and Organization along with supporting elemental data and associated content.

3. Create/Validate Processes—The hierarchy of Processes, now that the Reference and Infrastructure is in place, may be further developed to a level of granularity that existing, defined, and agreed procedures would support. The intent of this Guide has been to drive compliance from the

Business Influences and Compliance Model down to the lowest level process, or work instruction. Creating new processes, or validating current processes, is a major step in that process and has a significant impact.

During the creation of the process environment, however, one should consider the following:

a. Establish a Collaborative Environment—One of the most effective ways of creating processes is to utilize infrastructure that will assist in online collaboration. While the undertaking of the creation activity could occur in several ways, it is most effective to use Process Management application software to provide online prototyping of a process as the discussion progresses. These tools not only provide a visualization of the process flow during creation but aid in the accumulation of information about the process and its activities. The information may include process purpose, description, influences, inputs and outputs, owner plus any available data such as activity description, instructions, inputs, outputs, executor, data, content, roles and applications. Where available provide any additionally defined links and inter-process and intra-process relationships that are required for continuing compliance. Of course, all of this information is subject to validation as the processes are worked through on a level-by-level basis.

b. Ensure Competent Attendees—Proper selection and preparation of attendees is important to the successful conduct of a process creation session. The selected attendees must have a good awareness of the Guide as a whole, where they fit into the picture, and the importance of their taking part and making a substantive contribution. Remind them that it is the tacit knowledge of their environment that is important to the exercise. Having applicable Reference information and a robust infrastructure in place prior to the sessions significantly facilitates the accumulation of their contribution. In addition, making the resultant process-work available on the network immediately after the sessions provides them with a sense that the Guide is real and has momentum.

c. Identify Opportunities—During the translation of the Business Influences, opportunities will become evident. Some of them may find their way into the Process Creation/Validation sessions while others are identified during those sessions. The latter are entered on the list of processes to address or reconcile against the Influence Translation process for further clarification.

Several years ago, someone coined the phrase "low hanging fruit." The phrase described the obvious opportunities for obtaining high ROI within an organization. At this point, the Solution Center Team should look for these opportunities and gauge their importance in relation to ECM as a whole. They include Business Influences not identified or translated to Influence or Operation Management functions; Function Scenarios either not identified or unclear; Hierarchy of Governance compliance neither established nor traceable; Processes missing, not agreed on, and/or not implemented; Technology Opportunities systems and/or infrastructure not integrated; and/or needed capabilities not implemented. Since "low hanging fruit" are easy pickings, do not let that tide overwhelm the need to address opportunities of equal, but more effort-laden importance. If the latter are not addressed than there is a good chance that the implementation as a whole will not yield the expected benefits. Beware of statistical assurances that mask the true progression of the work.

d. Validate Process Coverage—At this point in the implementation, there should be a validation assessment to ensure the identification of all processes required to manage the business. Additionally, it is helpful to review the symptoms of message inundation discussed previously, i.e., paper, effort, media, and messages, to determine if these inefficiencies have been addressed with either new or improved processes.

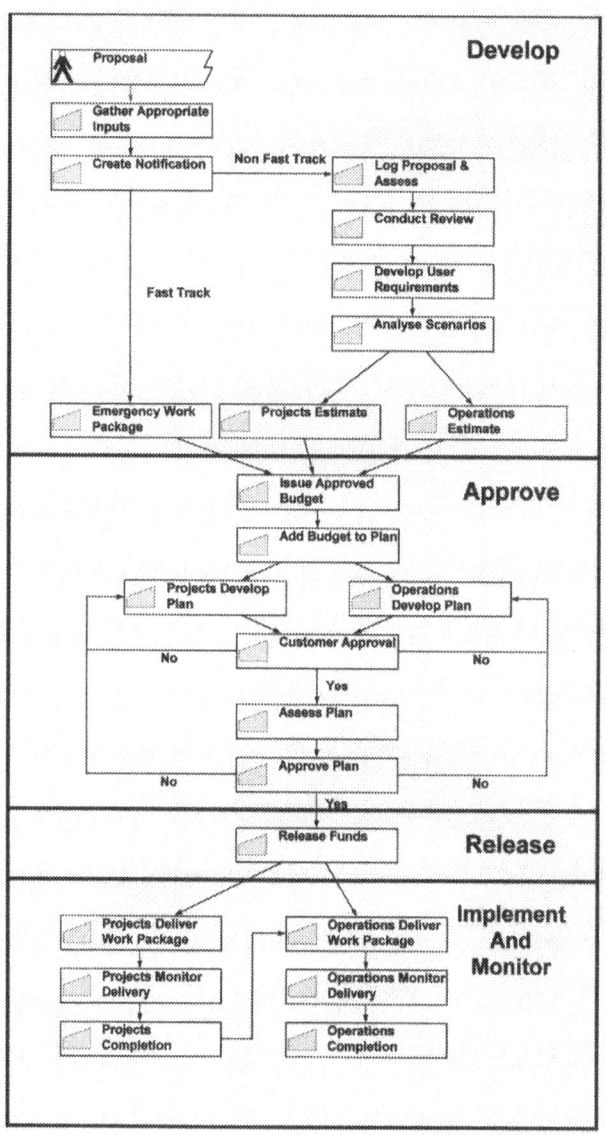

*Figure 9—Capital Project Management Scenario Example*

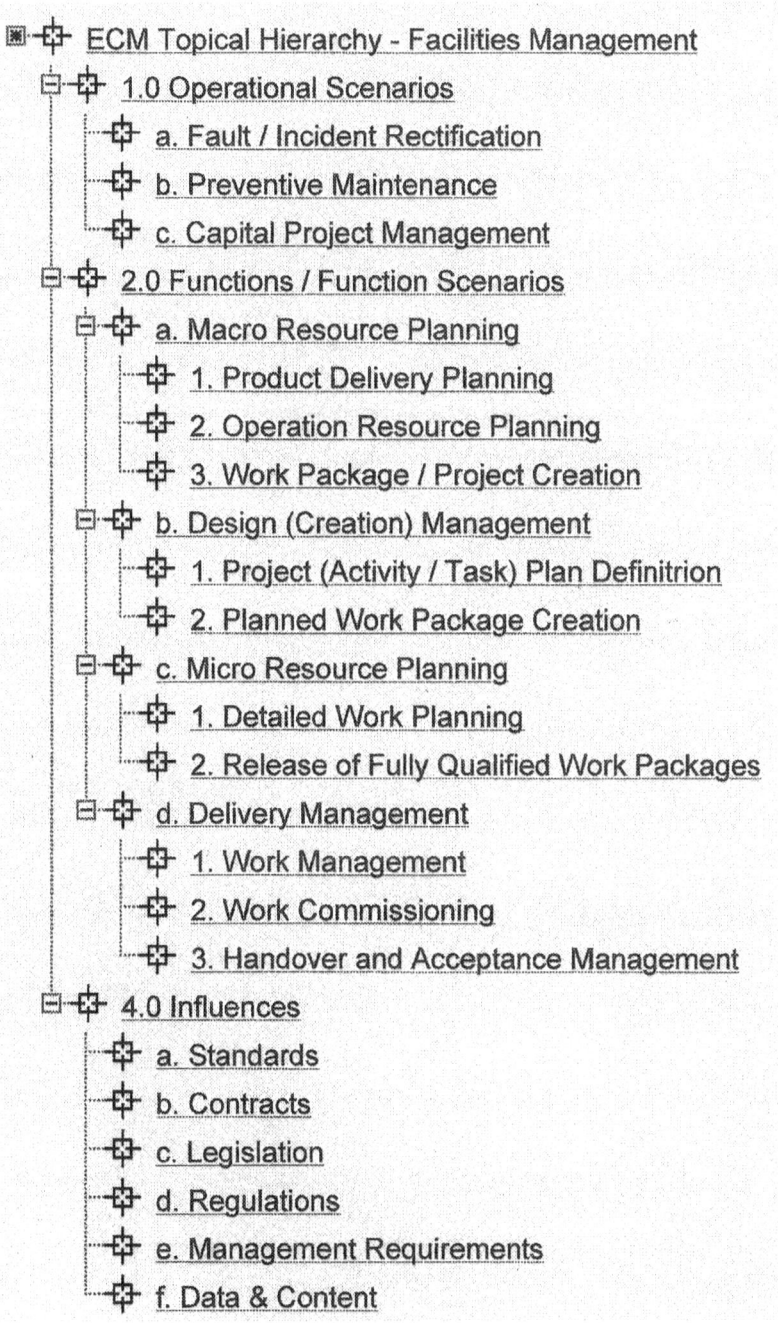

*Figure 10—Topic Hierarchy Example*

## Optimize/Automate Processes

The following six steps comprise the Optimization and/or Automation of processes phase of the implementation:

1. Review Processes—The optimization of a process may be as simple as taking the time to review the purpose of the process with the primary consumer to assure its compliance with the Business Influences and Scenarios. Review of processes, activities, and their associated roles may yield marginal to significant increases in productivity and/or lead to process change. During discussions with users, it is important to assure that the emphasis placed upon the requirements for the process is consistent across all users. Finance, for example, may wish to pride itself in saving the company money by reducing inventory. However, the techniques employed may adversely affect production and therefore revenue. Address inconsistencies, such as the one described in this example. If they are not accommodated earlier in the implementation, they must be addressed during the Influence Translation Process.

2. Propose a Solution—If there is a requirement for process change, there may be a variety of available solutions. Identify owner, purpose, description, benefits, and anticipated cost and effort for each solution.

3. Simulate Proposed Solution—Once the definition of processes is complete and roles, occurrences, and timings identified, the process is a candidate for simulation in the Solution Center environment to assess its state of optimization. This will assist in the understanding of any impact on the make-up and distribution of the organization staffing, as well as application software and its effect on other processes. Simulation is a tool generally utilized as an aid in estimating resource requirements. The capability is available from some of the commercially accessible process prototyping packages. Preparation for simulation is important and the results should not be taken as definitive without applying some common sense.

4. Assess Automation—As with simulation, apply common sense prior to rushing to automation. Automation is a powerful tool which, if applied properly, can bring significant rewards such as the reduction of effort and time as well as timely feedback from exceptions. The latter facilitates focused attention on issues that should be of interest to management.

5. Automate—Utilizing Workflow, BPM, or existing business system capabilities, automation facilitates the processing of tasks/activities. Some

automated processes come as part of an existing or newly implemented business system, while others may require the application of workflow or BPM in order to be automated. Either way, automation can provide the dynamic feedback required to show compliance with metrics derived from the Business Influences. One of the outputs of process automation is the detail accumulated during the progress of the business system or workflow-supported processes. These details provide feedback on performance, identify when things go wrong, etc. This feedback (*See Figure 2, Influence Management Process Overview*) is the key to the closed-loop management of the Compliance environment.

## Establish Ongoing Compliance

Provisions made during the creation of the Reference and Infrastructure environments support the documentation and linking of the Business Influences with other elements such as requirements, processes, documents, and data. The definition of these elements and the implementation of a robust software application and communications infrastructure is the best way to accomplish this. Next, the discussion of the Business Influences and their identification and translation takes place. The result of this forms the catalyst to help achieve continuing compliance.

Once the Compliance Environment is established and the organization and processes are in place for its maintenance, consistent review of the following two areas will help assure its continued success:

a.  Influences, Scenarios, and Processes—Whenever an Influence, Scenario, or Process changes, the effect could ripple through the organization. Changes may range from fundamental, e.g., major changes, to health and safety legislation, to a cosmetic change classed as minor. Major changes could affect the whole of the organization, their ramifications understood and the results of that understanding incorporated throughout. Cosmetic changes too are incorporated to assure the compliance process is universal and cannot be suspect.

b.  Administration—Whenever there is a change to the administration of the ECM environment, the effect evaluated and compensation given to the appropriate processes. This is especially important because a breakdown here affects the ongoing credibility and viability of ECM.

## Validate Ongoing Compliance

Compliance is an integral part of everyone's job. It is important therefore that ECM continues as part of the fabric of the organization, not as a separate or piecemeal initiative. Throughout this Guide, the design of each phase was intended to move us a step closer to Continuing Compliance. It is now time for the entire team to regroup and ensure that the processes that support the compliance environment continue to remain solidly in place.

# Lessons Learned

## Introduction

The following illustrative, real life examples were not included in the ECM Guide text in order to keep that section crisp and easy to follow. In addition, many of the examples are cross-reference-able to a number of topics within the Guide. It was felt that the inclusion of the examples within the Guide would make it too busy and significantly increase its length. A summarization of these examples follows:

1. Not Invented Here (NIH)—Cross industry fertilization
2. We are here to help!
3. Underused or Misused, System and Technology Capabilities
4. System and Technology Capabilities Uniquely Leveraged

## Not Invented Here (NIH)—Cross industry fertilization

Many vertical industries tend to embrace parochial views of their environments. Often one hears that a certain industry is "different and complex," with the assertion that no other industry experiences the same difficulties when applying business concepts or systems. These cloistered views often prevent one industry from utilizing the experience gained in another.

"Different and complex" is often a symptom of the real culprit, the "Not invented here" syndrome. The syndrome, surprisingly sometimes found in high technology environments, often prevents one industry from utilizing available knowledge from another. Many times software companies take advantage of this syndrome and "package" mostly conventional software to address these specific needs. Obviously, they charge accordingly.

When it comes right down to it, in many cases one finds that the difficulty in identifying a solution is nothing more than semantics. In addition, there is often a little "don't rock my boat" influence from IT. There are also the many concerns which emerge when an efficient proposal is presented to the firm's consultancy/audit company.

One lesson to learn here is to be aware of the holistic needs of the business and challenge why the capability has not been addressed somewhere else with conventional, integrated software applications. Certainly, the consultancy and/or solution provider of "niche" software does not want its customers to manage with something off the shelf. Off-the-shelf software obviously lacks mysticism, and the associated inflated prices for implementation and service.

## Healthcare

The Management Information Systems (MIS) Manager of a large hospital complex received a challenge to help the hospital address issues of noncompliance. Most hospital systems at the time were mainframe based and took significant resources, e.g., time, money, and effort, to specify, develop, deliver, and make operational changes to the "system." The MIS manager did not have the time, the resources, or the money to address the situation through the conventional route.

Instead of taking the usual step of addressing the symptom, the MIS manager spent some time researching the problem and found that it was more complex than expected. In that regard, the requirements for an application solution increased substantially. Constrained by time and the lack of programming resources, the manager reviewed the processes underlying the opportunity and found that, based on previous experience, they were similar to those addressed by others using a conventional ERP system.

The implementation team selected a flexible off-the-shelf business application system. They tested the Influences, Scenarios, Processes, and Products against the software utilizing a Solution Center. The result was the modification of five screen prompts, e.g., Bill of Material became Physicians Preference List, and the application implemented in record time.

Soon after the implementation and the validation of the semantics translation, the same system addressed several additional opportunities such as doctor billing, accounts payable, etc. The decision, at least in that hospital complex, became a winner. A synergistic solution to a symptomatic opportunity solved by an open mind.

The solution made news in the healthcare world and was soon reviewed by a major US hospital management company. While there was significant interest from the user community, the IT Director indicated that the solution did not operate in their expensive legacy mainframe environment. His IT focused recommendation was to scrap the initiative. The board did not have the means to challenge him and provided with no other alternative, reluctantly honored his decision.

Comments:

The MIS Manager had enough common sense to know that the solution to his challenge was not unique and that semantics were a major inhibitor. His view was that someone in the supply chain vertical industry must have addressed the requirement previously.

The initiative was driven by a fluke in the industry, time to comply The MIS Manager's business-oriented approach, a unique quality in an MIS Manager, provided a sound foundation from which to start. His understanding of the hospital's Business Influences, Compliance Model, Scenarios, and Processes provided him with the requirements for the application solution and the roadmap to a successful implementation.

The year was 1985—some advanced out-of-the-box thinking for a time when IT managers measured success by the number of their employees and the size of their mainframes. Today, even though the technology has changed, size still matters. The more money a person spends, the bigger the salary—good business sense rarely seems to be part of the discussion.

## Facilities Management

The Facilities Management Director of a large Service Provision organization received a challenge to the fundamental precepts of his industry. Was the company an Asset Management company or a Service Provider that administered assets as part of the provision of its service?

The Director organized a team to review the company's Business Influences, Compliance Model, and Scenarios in order to understand the product it was marketing and its deployment. Of interest and considerable influence was the industry notion, fostered by a variety of asset-management software vendors and industry internal die-hard NIH purveyors that niche Asset Management application software was the solution and management should forget about the investigation and get on with the implementation.

On inspection of the company's service provision contracts, asset administration was seen to be only one of the provision requirements stipulated. Customer, service, training, transportation, catering, supply chain provision, and scheduling and management were also requirements in many of their over 250 customer sites. Robust service provision was paramount to customer satisfaction and therefore commercial success. Failure to perform was not a commercially viable option.

The traditional asset management software that was proposed did not address the full concept of Service Provision as a primary capability; therefore, it would have been the wrong choice. In addition, as the company managed services in hundreds of locations, the locally focused software's asset hierarchy requirement constrained the organization's flexibility.

After substantial discussions, the Director subsequently determined that Service Provision capabilities rather than traditional Asset Management capabilities were of greater importance for contract compliance. The resulting solution, based upon the top down approach, allowed them to implement previously purchased off-the-shelf software capabilities that would have otherwise become maintenance burdened "shelf-ware."

Comments:

These were perceptions that the team had to overcome:

1. The software solution had to be a "best of breed" Asset Management system because that's what they had been told by the industry and the purveyors of "niche" software;

2. The semantics of a conventional, non-niche business system would be too overwhelming for the customers to accept; and,

3. The insistence of the purveyor of the conventional ERP system that their system "didn't work that way," another cloistered view which delayed progress.

In spite of the difficulties, the team persevered and, after finding that the software purveyor's lack of support resulted from the fear that there would be a reduction in the number of licenses, decreased the consultancy commitment and implemented the system themselves.

In short, identifying and understanding the influences that defined how the company was required to operate changed the way the company viewed its product. The solution supported a step change that put the company at the forefront of the industry and allowed them to take on business that they would not have otherwise been able to absorb.

## Business Process Outsourcing

Those who have a background in manufacturing, construction, or other industries which for years have had the "make or buy," or "self perform or subcontract" option, will no doubt recognize the fundamentals of the new wave of Business Process Outsourcing (BPO). BPO has almost become a service industry of its own, helping many businesses make outsourcing decisions for administration processes that they have made so many times in the past for operation processes.

Is the new wave really so new, or is it yet another semantics based badge for something that is already known and perfected in many industries? Probably the latter, as there are few process opportunities that are "new" in business.

What are the challenges to address before one can outsource?

1   Definition of the scope of the process to be outsourced;

2   Assurance that the process to be outsourced is robust and bulletproof to minimize the chance of transferring an inefficient environment;

3   Validation that the competence of the supplier (sub-contractor) is sufficient to effectively manage the process and produce the product;

4   And, comfort that outsourcing will better the business as a whole.

Comments:

Over the years, Supply Chain Practitioners have refined Outsourcing decisions on a daily basis. Now their applicability has been translated to back office activities that were once held internally and are now open to the same scrutiny. So, is this a new wave or a lot of splash in the same water? Customer Relationship Management used to be Service Management. Supplier Relationship Management used to be Supplier Audits and Incoming Inspection. Are there others?

Opportunities like these become apparent during the Influence Identification and Translation activities of ECM. Understanding the total affect of influences on the business and leveraging internal as well as external capabilities by reducing the impact of semantics and "thinking outside the box" places management in a position to judge the optimal sourcing position for the organization. Logic, rather than the lure of quick profits, should prevail. Then again, we seem to be driven more by financial numbers these days rather than the services we provide to our customers.

## We are here to help:

Many people have cause to be suspicious when a consultancy company assures them that they are "here to help." The sentiment is often received with the same impact as if the Internal Revenue had made the announcement. However, business after business takes on major "optimization" projects, sold at board level since they involve so much money, because they fear that by not doing so they will be put the company at "risk." In fact, much of the money squandered on these projects has little to do with the ultimate goal and as such hits the bottom line with no more value than revenue for the consultants. The following are some illuminating examples:

## The POW Camp

Be aware of consultancy tendencies to break down the proverbial elephant into bitable chunks without first agreeing upon an understanding of the elephant as a whole and how the chunks relate.

Eating the elephant a bite at a time is a concept used by many to break down a large job into palatable chunks, the latter often identified as Pieces Of Work or POW. In some parts of the consulting world, a POW is equivalent to a 4-6 week assignment for one person. Their view is this is a customer salable charge, a palatable budget hit devised by the POW camp commandant, to add revenue to one or more of his company's consultancy practices. Often, the proposal of a POW addresses a symptom and not a problem, the presentation shrouded with emotion and the fear of risk and generally influencing the customer to authorize the POW to assure that he or she will be "safe."

Once established, the members of the POW Camp, assisted by the camp commandant, tend to grow quickly, feeding on the business one POW at a time. Many times, while accomplishing these individual tasks the original purpose of the effort falls into obscurity and the constituents focus on their separate tasks, fragmenting their efforts even more and leaving bits and pieces in their wake. This fragmentation eventually drains the business's resources, having the same effect as a POW camp in a military campaign. Eventually the business wakes up and realizes the excessive cost, culls the program, and relieves the camp commandant of his or her command.

Undaunted, the commandant returns to the practice for a huddle. There, with the assistance of partners and other resources, he or she creates a proposal to correct the less than optimal use of customer funds. Sadly, management accepts many of the revised proposals because they feel that they have no alternative, the POW camp is slowly reinstated and the cycle begins again.

Comments:

The camp commandant's focus is on increasing revenue and keeping the picture of the elephant obscure. It is much like someone hiding the puzzle box cover and some of the pieces when one is trying to complete a puzzle. While this maneuver generates income for the consultancy, it drains the coffers of the business and many times provides little value and a lot of added effort.

Digging the hole deeper by retaining the same consultancy organization after they have been discharged, ostensibly because they "know" the business "and it will be cheaper the second time around," only prepares the company for the third time around, and so on.

Managing the Compliance Model (the Puzzle box cover), Influences, Scenarios, Processes, and Products required to operate the business assists in reducing the fragmentation efforts of a POW camp.

## Silver Belts

The trend to roll out Six Sigma across organizations as the new savior obviates the need for revisiting the fundamental job requirements of yesteryear. There was a time when these techniques were part of my education and their application expected as part of my job. If I utilized them successfully, when they were required, then I usually managed to keep my job.

Those individuals from the past who managed to keep their jobs may be reverently referred to, in the context of Six Sigma, as Silver Belts. The question is what happened? Possibly, the fact that fewer and fewer individuals seem to be "apprenticed" and therefore do not have a hands-on understanding of the fundamentals that support the business and the firsthand application of Six Sigma principles, and similar types of techniques. "Hands-On" Apprenticeship training could provide experience that would support the automatic initiation and use of these techniques as a practitioner. Sadly, "Hands-On Apprenticeships have not been in vogue for years.

Packaging is probably another answer with the creation and marketing of a structured guide that utilizes these techniques. What it really boils down to is consultancy, the sale of existing and known information to someone that should know it. Instead of offering the initiative as a refresher, consultancies sell it as an end goal, focusing on gathering low hanging fruit that many times may be a symptom rather than the problem.

This is in no way critical of the new waves that spring up now and then. There is obviously a need and Six Sigma is filling it. The question is why is it necessary to implement Six Sigma from a total business standpoint, rather than some other standard or guide such as ISO, TQM, or one of the many flavors of the day/Japanese-named concepts that have sprung up over the years. (Sadly, Joshiki is rarely among them.) These concepts should be part of the fabric of the business, supported by each employee's toolkit.

Comments:

Over the years, we have found that little is new in the fundamentals of the business of running the business. Techniques, many times facilitated by technology, certainly emerge as facilitators of what would otherwise be difficult tasks. Often the branding of these techniques is simply the semantics that separate what they do from what formerly existed. Many times this confuses the business. Maybe that is the intention, as it helps sell seminars, training, certifications, and consultancy.

Focusing on the business as a whole through the identification and translation of Business Influences helps to pinpoint where optimization is required. Understanding the need and the ultimate deliverable provides the basis for determining the technique, or techniques, utilized to implement the optimization. Starting with the technique as an end goal is often the equivalent of looking through the wrong end of a telescope. This is another reason for the creation of the ECM Guide, to act as a reality check whenever "end game flavor of the month" initiatives are proposed.

# Underused, or Misused, System and Technology Capabilities:

Companies purchase business systems for the best of reasons. However, some systems, or modules thereof, are never installed and become known as "shelf-ware." They sit on a sometimes-virtual shelf to collect maintenance charges. Others are implemented, but due to inappropriate-use and/or inefficient and ineffective implementations—many times resulting in "scope crimp"—they do not provide the originally marketed results.

Inappropriate use, however, is often a big culprit. Sometimes, individual managers will utilize the "system" in an attempt to attain their individual goals. This often occurs when there is differing emphasis assigned during the translation of Business Influences. As a result, what is good for one function may not necessarily be good for another and, while each may be meeting its goals, one or the other, or both, could be adversely affecting the business as a whole.

Inefficient or ineffective implementations often happen when many of the resources, such as time, effort, and funds, consumed during the creation of the "feel good factor" and Risk Register result in precious little resources left for implementation. Sadly, in many cases, it is the IT Director/CIO who must return to plead for more money from the management coffers after the initial consultancy drain has overspent the authorized budget.

### Transportation Management

A transportation company's board of directors, convinced of the need for fiscal compliance, authorized a fixed price project to replace its aging, non-integrated, and less than functional financial, procurement, and fixed asset systems. The consulting firm that proposed the project expended a considerable amount of money early in the exercise to establish that "feeling good factor" and the Risk Register (the latter of which is sometimes called the "Bible of Blame") in case things do not turn out as planned.

As the implementation progressed, the money soon ran low and the task became daunting. As is usually the case in situations like this, the program manager was replaced by another who quickly, and with much fanfare, brought the implementation to a "successful" close.

Not long after the "successful, on-time, and on-budget" implementation was announced, "opportunities" began to arise. Consumers noticed that the activation of the purchasing requisition system, one of the primary reasons for the new business system initiative, had not happened. Other aspects of the initiative, like the Fixed Asset system sorely needed in an asset-based company, were now relegated to "Phase 1". In fact, many other capabilities were now relegated to "Phase 1" due to "scope crimp" and the paid for but unused software for the yet to be planned and budgeted "Phase 1" had become "shelf-ware", collecting maintenance fees. In addition, the capabilities which had been available in the previous legacy system environment had, in many cases, been curtailed. The reason given was the lack of time and money to complete the initiative as originally specified.

Obviously, there were some benefits; there always is when a single system replaces several systems that are not integrated and have poor functionality. The difference between what happened and what could have happened is the real cost of "scope crimp."

Comments:

One might ask how this could happen. The answer to that consists of multiple parts:

a.  Business Influences—There was no overall Compliance Model to assure a common goal. The implementation, driven by Finance, was to achieve a common chart of accounts. The fact that Operations needed an automated purchase requisition as well as fixed asset capability to have a reasonable chance of running the business became secondary.

b.  Management—The consultancy firm, poorly managed, received carte blanche status by default. Human Resources, not wanting to upset anyone along the way, supported the consultancy firm's lavish expenditure on the "feeling good factor." By the time the money had started running out, both the consultancy company and management started covering their proverbial tracks by marketing success without letting the consumer know that they were receiving less than originally promised.

c.  Effectiveness—There are always benefits in the implementation of an integrated environment. It sets the stage for expanding the future use of systems and the further reduction of disparate legacy systems. In the short term, however, there were drawbacks: the number of financial manual processes increased; the number of individuals who could access the financial system for information to accomplish their work decreased; and the number of reports generated to compensate for the lack of access...increased significantly.

The implementation was, in some respects, a success. However, from a value added standpoint it fell way short of the intended mark. It is obvious that the emphasis from finance overwhelmed the needs of operations and, in this case, continued to place the business at risk due to a very inaccurate asset register. The "White Paper" that was subsequently published to extol the accomplishments of the company, the consultancy supplier, and the team obscured the shortcomings of the implementation.

## Service Management

Armed with the Transportation Management Company's "White Paper of Success," if it could be called white, the same consultancy company approached a service management company. They extolled their own virtues at board level while waving the "white" paper as proof of their success. The consultancy promised the same success, and as a result, it secured a lucrative contract to accomplish the deliverables originally promised to the Transportation Management Company.

You can probably guess what happened next. The eventual result was the same with one exception—the implementation cost was double the Transportation Management Company's "estimate" and, as before, many of the capabilities specified for the implementation were again relegated to the infamous "Phase 1", some even to the newly invented "Phase 2".

Comments:

It is fascinating that well-educated and experienced board directors could be lulled into a false sense of security by a consultancy company's sales tactics. The company could have averted much of what happened if they had established their needs utilizing the concepts of ECM. That would have provided them with an environment with which they could challenge the consultancy company's efforts and manage the project's scope, potentially saving them a significant amount of money.

## Materials Management

Sometimes Business Influences that seem to be common across several functions may be detrimental if not applied equally to the business as a whole. For example, the need to maintain an optimal inventory is paramount for many businesses. However, if the company does not understand and agree on the effect of an initiative to reduce inventory across the business, then disaster could occur.

Let us look at the example of the Materials Manager who, armed with a bonus-laced goal, decides to drive the inventory to zero. This is exactly what happened in one hospital environment when inventory, reduced so much that surgical trays were not available to the trauma operating rooms, caused the nurses to "borrow" trays from a neighboring hospital. This informal variation of "just-in-time" masked their lack of inventory for some time until the "borrowed" inventory variance caused havoc with the other hospital's operating rooms. The provisioning hospital's materials manager was eventually admonished for his lack of attention to detail.

Meanwhile back at the borrowing hospital, the Material's Manager received his bonus for his excellent achievement; management being unaware of the external effects of the initiative. In addition, management had ignored the unhappy staff who had complained to them about the lack of inventory. Eventually the same union that the hospital administration had been successfully keeping at bay for some time organized the staff. Within a short period the level of inventory, as well as the staff's salaries and benefits, soon rose.

Comments:

Validate the focused application of goals with other Business Influences during their translation. Problems resulting from inconsistencies, as the requirements ripple down from the Business Scenarios through to the Processes, will become obvious and should provide feedback for reconciliation to the Influence Translation process. Obviously, this continuous reconciliation of processes process is important to the well being of the business.

Just as a note, the reduction of inventory, effort, etc., is everyone's goal and should not be compensated within one manager's bonus. Just-In-Time beats Just-Too-Late any day.

## System and Technology Capabilities Uniquely Leveraged:

The purpose of a software application tool is to help increase one's productivity. Some, however, may disagree and perceive it as more of a burden. In many instances, as shown in the previous examples, they are right. There are times though when organizations uniquely leverage business system technology capabilities for the betterment of the business. The following are a few examples:

### Vertically Integrated Manufacturing Management

Why should it require an IT department to specify, purchase, implement, and maintain a business system in this high-tech age of user-oriented capabilities? Almost twenty years ago, it happened successfully and uniquely. Not many would believe this.

"I want a business system implemented that will integrate my operations," the president said as he lit his cigar. "Currently, the downstairs (physical) inventory does not match the upstairs (book) inventory. I need one that provides me with timely and correct answers. Oh, by the way, I want it implemented in all the divisions within two years. Here is your salary and stock option. Have we got a deal?" he asked the prospective IT director.

"Sounds good to me," the prospect replied.

"There's just one other requirement," the president challenged.

"What's that?" the prospect asked, perplexed.

"You can't have an IT department," the president replied. "We don't have one now and I don't want one."

"If that's what you want then I'll make it happen," the prospect replied.

Three months later, in the summer of 1985, the Business System was chosen and negotiations began. Two weeks later the project started and within nine months, the first plant of the four-division, vertically integrated corporation went online. One year later, financial trial balances were running on a weekly basis, making the previous end of period P&L fiasco redundant.

What happened? Easy: power transferred to the people. Module Administrators, chosen from each of the major site functions, took charge of and implemented the flexible consumer-oriented business system. After competence assessment and training, they implemented in record time.

Unlike conventional implementations, the Module Administrators took complete control of the environment, from cold starting the computer to managing security, the database, screens, and processes for their areas. The team acted as one and in that regard, was self-policing. One would question whether the same capability exists with today's "state-of-the-art" systems!

Two years later, due to technology and market shifts, the company went out of business. The refined the processes and systems that ran the company were utilized to optimize the remaining contracts build-out, providing management with their last, and significant, bonus.

Comments:

This is the first time I had applied ECM concepts across a corporation. The emphasis placed on the need for the identification and translation of Influence requirements ensured the inclusion of each of the internal and external influencers at each of the plants. The success of the initiative, and the user-maintained environment it created, continues in the minds of those who were involved. What is strange is the business system product did not do well in the marketplace. The reason: IT Directors of the time were paranoid about allowing users to do anything that was in their purview. It just was not good for their resume. I heard then, as I do today—"it's a security issue". One wonders whether we are dealing with a "state-of-the-art" or "state-of-the-ark" IT environment.

## Maritime Management

Sometimes it is to business's advantage to fatten their business system implementation costs. How could that happen, one might ask. Read the comments below about a Maritime Management company who had two opportunities.

The first opportunity was short-term, created by the union that operated their ports. The union demanded staff increases in each port to handle the additional infusion of paperwork caused by the increased throughput of containers at the gate. If they succeeded, it would have increased the company's costs in each port by a significant amount. It would also establish an industry precedent, a substantial risk to the industry as a whole.

The second, a much longer-term opportunity, involved a scheme to increase tariffs on the containers and goods they transported. The authorization for increases in tariffs was dependent upon increases in the capital expenditure required to support operations. In that respect, the company had to devise a plan to create the increase.

The Company decided on a two-pronged, but interrelated, approach. They designed the first approach to reduce risk. The second approach was to increase tariffs. Both, when successful, would have a positive effect on the bottom line.

The company felt that the short-term opportunity required immediate attention, as it was necessary to mitigate the risk of increasing staff at the gate. They knew that their current check-in system was manual, time-consuming, and fraught with error. The delays often caused overtime to handle the long tractor-trailer and container queues, many times tailing back onto heavily used streets—and sometimes freeways. The company had to pay double time for the drivers to wait in these queues and the cost had substantially increased over the years.

The short-term approach was necessary until the planned long-term solution could be developed and implemented. The approach involved implementing a central booking and local port capabilities to handle the gate and yard operations as well as stow, discharge, and ship stabilization. The task took a small team several months to develop and when the solution was ready, a port was chosen for the initial trials. Obviously, a successful implementation would have detrimental effects on the union's expansionist plan and cause significant reduction of the driver's overtime payments. In that regard, instead of a natural build-up of containers throughout the night of the trail, all the drivers banded together and arrived early, attempting to delay the inevitable.

Preparation won the day, or really, the evening. With the aid of the new system, several hundred containers moved through in record time. The capability allowed the gate staff to leave four hours early, much to their delight. The truckers and union management, however, were not pleased.

Prior to the inclusion of the risk reduction team, the company enlisted the aid of a well-known consultancy firm to advise them and manage the selection, development, and implementation of the ultimate solution. The mainframe-based design resulted in the purchase and installation of a mainframe immediately after the deployment of the risk reduction team. As the selection of ultimate solution software took over a year, the mainframe, with only its console connected, was nicknamed the World's Largest PC.

After significant research, the team purchased a software application solution of appropriate size and considerable price and the development work began. However, the project soon exceeded its budget, became seriously behind schedule, and was ultimately brought to a halt.

The consultancy company then disappeared for a while, regrouping as they do. Eventually they returned, declared the previous effort a disaster, and put forward a plan to start afresh. The board accepted the new plan and work began again. However, the second plan's budget quickly overran the project after a significant capital outlay the implementation was eventually completed. The anticipated result supported the application for, and the acceptance of, the welcomed tariff increase.

Comments:

This is an example of a well thought out plan to leverage IT for the financial benefit of the organization and at the same time ensure that the company did not set a precedence within the industry. The fact that it did not seem well-orchestrated and involved considerable cost only helped their cause, an option rarely available to a commercial organization.

## Put the responsibility back in Sales and Marketing's lap.

After the end of the month shipments have left the plant and the performance for the period is in progress, how many of you have heard the circular argument "I would have made or created more '___' (insert one of the following: shipments, product, orders) if someone else had done his or her job"?

For years, the monkey of responsibility has been placed on the shoulders of operations who have been consistently blamed for not reacting quickly enough no matter how little time they have to perform. The real responsibility could have been laid at the feet of planning, which has the responsibility for telling manufacturing what to do and when. However, planning only encompasses production planning and many times they are not provided reasonable input from major influences like sales and marketing. As a result, production could not ship the product produced.

The Director of Operations in one company finally had enough and approached the Materials Manager for relief. After some discussion, they agreed that the real nut to crack was optimization of the use of the limited capacity in final test. In order to optimize the plant around the testing facility, several major changes had to occur:

1. Sales and Marketing must be made responsible for the planning of Final Test;
2. The production line, instead of focusing on final product related work orders, would focus on providing sufficient components to the Final Test environment;
3. All configured finished goods and staged finished goods kits would be broken down to the pre-test level of component and either moved to the manufacturing floor stock or returned to stockroom inventory;
4. The end-of-month shipment mentality would change to an end-of-week shipment mentality.

After a month of effort, positive results began to emerge. The following is a summary:

The configured finished goods de-kitting and breakdown exercise yielded a significant amount of inventory. Some of the components filled the then current shortages while the balance caused a major reshuffle in the MRP, pushing out orders for purchased as well as manufactured parts. It is interesting that portions of the components released were old-revision and as a result reworked to make them usable or scrapped. With little remaining in the Finished Goods stockroom, the space was released to expand Final Test capacity.

The Final Test schedule was taken over by sales and marketing who determined and managed its capacity. They soon learned the difficulties of reprioritizing, and trying to keep the customer happy, and pressure brought to bear on the sales person to establish delivery based upon the customer's true needs rather than the date of their commission check.

The reshuffle reduced the actual order lead-time from ninety days to less than thirty. The end-of-the-month syndrome—shipping 80% of the month's shipments out on the last 24 hours of the month—changed to shipping 25% of the month's shipments every Friday.

Some of the results, classified as negative, should be tempered with the positive impact of the reorganization:

1. The company had to write down the value earned labor that charged to the finished goods. However, some of the finished goods had been in stock for months, taking up valuable inventory and space, their components sometimes holding up orders;

2. Some of the assembly kits and fabrication work orders brought in from the floor were several years old and cancelled, with the raw materials returned to raw materials stores. However, the personnel in the manufacturing area became suspicious that there would be no work for them, having taken solace in the pallets of work orders that littered the floor. To counter the apprehension, planning provided manufacturing personnel with a comprehensive picture of what was happening and they soon returned to work assured that their jobs were safe. It was interesting that the newly released "increase" in capacity allowed the company to increase sales and market by faster turnaround to the customer. Work in progress and inventory soon decreased and the thirteen expediters, who caused more harm than good by "stealing" parts from each other, were released back to assembly and now had to work for a living.

Comments:

This transformation would not have happened without the management and board of directors understanding the significant impact of the influences on their business. This provided them with a comprehensive picture with which they were able to reorient their responsibilities and make a stepchange to the efficiency of the plant.

## Application Engineering Management

There is a view by many boards that if a project is going to have a big impact on the business then it must be expensive, otherwise why would the board have to be involved? History, and those who would like to make a lot of consultancy money, has probably led boards to believe that this is true. Therefore, by default, it is. However, there are situations where "cheap and cheerful" solutions may provide a step change in the way a business operates, and the board should be involved. The following is a good example:

A global firm holding a major stake in the mechanical engineering marketplace was about to embark on an upgrade of its ICT infrastructure. To accomplish this they authorized a two-year expenditure of tens of millions of dollars of capital. The payback was marginal, fundamentally oriented at not falling any further behind the competition rather than providing a step change in the way the business operated.

Lost in the shuffle was the facility to provide global access, at the cost of a couple of thousand dollars per year and less than a thousand to install. It would provide low cost links between the engineering center's global virtual private network, or "cloud," and the rest of world. The capability provided access points to installations in over two hundred countries. Many of these were in remote locations.

After a significant amount of delay, mostly caused by the IT community, the first connection to the main engineering center was operational. What benefits did this low cost approach provide?

1. Information Access—Online access to applications information provided the latest optimized solutions to application engineers as well as customer maintenance management. Once an application solution was registered, it was available to all. This sharing of information meant applications were more consistent and a significant reduction in the then current re- re- re- and re-engineering effort expended worldwide on essentially the same requirement.

2. Documentation Translation—Documentation made available online reduced the need for the physical distribution of changed drawings to each of registered holders of those drawings, wherever they were in the world. As there was little feedback from the customers' maintenance personnel, the effort on their part to identify unneeded drawings and keep current with the paper mill was growing. Even if they were up to date with their filing, they would not know if the information on the drawing was the latest and had to make an international call to the engi-

neering center to find out. This process was unnecessary once the network access was available.

3. Technology Cost Transfer—In an effort to realize immediate payback for this solution, the implementation team convinced those who spent many hours on international telephone calls seeking information to switch to the computer. Internal users and customers were provided with laptops, communications access and application solution software, and office automation to conduct their business. Not only did the solution make them more efficient, it actually reduced the overall communications cost. Once the first implementation was effective, the word passed through the company, resulting in a deluge of requests for the same capabilities.

Comments:

Sometimes programs do not require a substantial outlay to effect a step change in the productivity of a business. Identification of these types of opportunities occurs during Business Influence Identification and Translation. These provide senior management with options of which they may well be unaware, especially when technology cost transfer will pay for them.

# In Conclusion

The reality of business today is that there is no aspect of external or internal forces which influence an enterprise can go unnoticed. More and more regulation, attention to security, privacy, health, safety, quality, and environment issues require that a robust and continuous compliance support environment be in place to safeguard the business, its employees, and the markets in which it is involved.

This is the goal of the ECM Guide: to facilitate the creation of a Continuously Compliant environment through the management of Business Influences and their effect on the enterprise. However, this is not always as easy as it seems, as competing factions within the business may, while seemingly flying a singular banner, be putting the business at risk.

That is why it is important to insure that:

1. all Business Influences are Identified and that there are processes in place to insure the identification of future additions and variants;

2. there are processes in place to support the prioritization of Business Influences and an understanding of their effect across the Business Functions;

3. the Business Scenarios accurately reflect the reason for being in business and the revenue products they produce, and that this environment is supported by robust processes;

4. the Business Functions are effectively organized and accurately reflect the internal products, or Business Scenario product components, that insure the continued success of the Enterprise;

5. the supporting Functional Scenarios and Processes, and their products, support the compliance requirements of the Enterprise.

These may seem ominous; however, meeting the challenge is a requirement if one expects to succeed in business.

As mentioned at the beginning, this Guide has taken many forms over the years and continues to evolve. I see this as the first formal edition and, in that regard, solicit your comments and ideas from its use and implementation to make the next edition a more robust tool for the practitioner. Drop by www.TheECM.com regularly for interim updates. I welcome your tactical inclusion. My email address is JJJF@TheECM.com .

# Appendices

## Introduction

These appendices contain examples and concepts referred to in the ECM Guide. Their content is illustrative rather than prescriptive and made available for three reasons:

1 to avoid reinventing the wheel each time this Guide is implemented, as sometimes a "clean sheet of paper" creates a blank;

2 to attempt a standardized approach where it is lacking or obscure;

3 to speed up the implementation of the Guide by providing structure that otherwise would have to be created from scratch.

# Appendix A—Business Influence examples

The following are a few examples of Business Influences. The examples below include inputs from a small sample of industries. In that respect, they are illustrative, not prescriptive.

Standards Examples:

European Foundation for Quality Management (EFQM)—
www.efqm.org
Information Technology Infrastructure Library (ITIL)—
www.ogc.gov.uk/index.asp?id=2261
International Organization for Standardization (ISO)—
www.iso.ch/iso/en/ISOOnline.frontpage
IT Governance Institute (ITGI)
www.ITGI.com

Contracts Examples:

In general, the information within contracts tends to be held privately. There are varieties of contract types: Customer, Public Private Partnerships (PPP), Publicly Financed Initiatives (PFI), Joint Ventures (JV), long-term suppliers, trading agreements, etc. However, the following are good, publicly available, examples of contracts:

Contractual Safety Case—
www.tubelines.com/docs/safety_case.pdf
Plant Safety Case—
www.tubelines.com/docs/transplant_case.pdf
Environmental Policy—
www.networkrail.co.uk/cache/Network%20Rail%20Env%20Policy.pdf

Legislation/Regulatory Examples:

    Governance:
        Sarbanes-Oxley Act (SOX) Act: Summary—
            www.aicpa.org/info/sarbanes_oxley_summary.htm
    Human Resources:
        Health Insurance Portability and Accountability Act (HIPAA)
            www.hhs.gov/ocr/hipaa/
    Health & Safety:
        UK Sites—
        Health and Safety Executive (HSE)—
            www.hse.gov.uk/
        US Sites—
            www.msdssearch.com/GovLinksN.htm

Management Requirements Examples:

These are generally specific to the business. Refer to your company's management requirements.

Data Examples:

Refer to your specific drivers for examples. The best way to start is to identify which data could cause noncompliance and therefore penalties.

Best Practice:

    Best Manufacturing Practices—
        www.bmpcoe.org/
    Best Practice LLC—
        www.best-in-class.com/
    Department of Trade and Industry Best Practice—
        www.dti.gov.uk/mbp/
    International Telecommunication Union (eTOM)—
        www.itu.int/ITU-T/studygroups/com04/tmc/etom/
    National Governors Association—
        www.nga.org/center/1,1188,00.html
    Office of Government Commerce—
        www.OGC.gov.uk
    Six Sigma—
        www.isixsigma.com/
    Supply Chain Council (SCOR)—
        www.supply-chain.org/

# Appendix B—Business/Function Scenario examples

## Business Scenario Examples

The following are a few vertical industry examples of Business Scenarios. They are illustrative, not prescriptive.

Service Management

> Fault/Incident Rectification
> Preventive Maintenance Management
> Capital Project Management

Manufacturing Management

> Order Management
> Manufacturing Management
> Fulfillment Management

Standards Management

> Needs Appreciation Management
> Standards Management
> Compliance Management

Transportation Management—Containers

> Booking Management
> Journey Management
> Yard Management
> Stow (Mount) and Discharge (Dismount) Management

# Appendix C—Elemental Standards examples

The following are examples of elemental standards. This is merely a sample and by no means a complete listing of all the possibilities. Agree on these before or early in the creation of the Solution Center.

Account—Coding, Structure
Product Number—Type, Classification
Customer Number—Type, Classification
Order Number—Type (Purchase, Work, Project, Sales)
Employee Number—Type (Internal, External, etc.), Classification (Role)
Asset Number—Type, Classification
Location—Building, Room, etc.
Organization—Department, Division, Group, etc.
Tax Codes

# Appendix D—Information Providers

The following is an illustrative list of professional bodies and organizations that provide further information relating to the Enterprise Compliance Management concept and various application solution providers. This list is by no means exhaustive.

AIIM International—www.AIIM.org
Association of Business Process Management Professionals—
    www.abpmp.org
BPM Institute—www.BPMinstitite.org
BPR Online Learning—www.prosci.com
BrainStorm Group, Business Management Conferences—
    www.brainstorm-group.com/bsgweb/index.asp
Business.com—BPM—
www.business.com/directory/management/management_consulting/
    business_process/
Business.com—Content—
www.business.com/search/rslt_default.asp?r4=t&query=content
Business Process Management Group—www.BPMG.org
Business Process Management Initiative—www.BPMI.org
Business Process Trends—www.bptrends.com
Butler Group—Analysts—www.ButlerGroup.com
CFO Magazine—www.CFO.com
CIO Magazine—www.CIO.com
Conspectus—IT Magazine—www.Conspectus.com
Cutter IT Journal—www.cutter.com/itjournal
Darwin—IT Magazine—www.DarwinMag.com
Gartner Group—Analysts—www.Gartner.com
INFORMS—Institute for Operations Research and Management
    Sciences—www.informs.org
MIT Technology Review—www.TechnologyReview.com
Workflow Management Coalition—www.WfMC.org

# Appendix E—Semantics

Alert—a message, automatically generated by the business system, Business Process Management, or workflow, indicating a predetermined event has occurred.

Best Practice—Evident in many concepts such s SCOR, eTOM, etc. Be aware that it sometimes refers to the "Best" a consultancy "Practice" can manage. It is therefore important to confer with sources other that your consultancy company before accepting their recommendations out of hand. In other words, it is your responsibility to do your homework.

Bible of Blame—a phrase that is attributable to consultants, describing their effort to shift the blame from themselves to the client using Risk and Issues Registers. The register lists those customers informed of possible risks or issues, who should have dealt with them, and therefore who should not be surprised when they occur. Frequently, a considerable amount of effort and money spent on these registers early in the project causes them to be predisposed.

Business Function—a high-level group of Influence Management or Operation related activities that provide a suite of capabilities supporting a certain aspect of the business. Functions are major components of the Compliance Model and contain Scenarios that create complete internal products, e.g., paid invoice, or components of a final product, e.g., application design.

Business Influences—provide the reasons for a business's existence. Examples of these are contracts, trading agreements, etc. These may also be the factors by which the business is operated, such as standards, regulations, etc.

Business Influence Translation—the translation of Business Influences into products created by processes and managed by Influence and Operation Management.

Business Scenario—is a high-level end-to-end Information Management or Operation process that produces a revenue product. Business Scenarios overlay more than one Business Function, utilizing each function's capabilities to varying degrees. Typically, a business operates on fewer than five Business Operation Scenarios. The scenarios are generally unique to the conduct of a vertical industry and the product or service it delivers. (*See Appendix B*)

CIO—Chief Information Officer.

Compliance Model—is a high-level graphical representation depicting the relationship between each of the components that manage a business enterprise. *See Figure 1* for a view of the Compliance Model used throughout this work.

Content—consists of all forms of information including text, formatted text such as HTML pages, interactive and/or dynamic Web page images, animation, video, and sound files.

Delivery Management—ensures the competent and complete delivery of the Fully Qualified Work Package.

Design—(sometimes called "Create") translates the proposed work packages/projects onto fully qualified work packages/projects and plans for their execution.

Detailed Work Planning—Once the creation of the project plan and planned work package(s) has taken place, it is time for the initiation of the detailed work plan. This will identify the sequence of the package's task implementation.

Elemental Information—core data, content, and software application information required to operate the business effectively.

Enterprise Compliance Management (ECM)—is a Guide that facilitates the identification and translation of compliance requirements to Influence and Operation Management Processes utilizing optimized Message Media.

Function Scenario—a high-level end-to-end process that occurs within a Function. In some cases, the title of a Function Scenario may be synonymous with the name of a Function, e.g., Payable Processing.

Function—Functions tend to be departments or groups that produce an internal product.

Influence—See Business Influence

Influence Management (IM)—The management of Influence requirements generated by external and internal organizations.

Influencers—Internal or external organizations that create compliance requirements.

Information Supply Chain (ISC)—is the total path from the consumer requirement for information, through intervening agents, to the ultimate supplier of that information.

Handover and Acceptance Management—Making sure the product meets the specification is often quite different from the finalization of the paperwork and transfer of ownership. However, both are important for the successful utilization of the product produced.

Joshiki—a rarely used Japanese concept, meaning "everlasting knowledge," translated to the West as "common sense."

KISS—Keep It Simple, Stupid

Message—a Message should be structured data passed from sender to receiver via Message Media. Structure should include specific data required to minimize the effort associated with message processing.

Message Media—any delivery medium such as paper, e-mails, fax, SMS, etc., or management medium such as business systems, workflow, etc., that is utilized to deliver or manage messages.

Macro-Resource Planning—translates the identified requirements of Influence Management into high-level work packages/projects. In the heat of daily requirements, Micro-Resource Planning could easily receive the preponderance of effort if it is necessary to "get the product out the door," but it is certainly detrimental to the continued viability of the business.

Micro-Resource Planning—Micro-Resource Planning schedules, at a detailed level, resources for the Planned Work Package/Project Plan and releases Fully Qualified Work Packages/Sub Projects for execution.

NIH—Not Invented Here.

Operation Resource Planning—the management of all resources across the Operation environment.

Piece of Work (POW)—a consultancy unit of measure equaling the effort of one consultant for four to six weeks, the cost of which is thought to be just below the budget threshold of the target customer. POWs are saleable commodities in the consultancy world and often expand into large camps.

Planned Work Package Creation—The work package should be associated with each project activity/task for the accumulation of costs, time, and effort. The package should tie back to the business case, project plan, and tendering activities to complete the feedback loop.

Portal—provides consumer managed access to repository information.

Process Coordinator—is the focal point of the ECM Guide who manages a process across either a Business or Function Scenario. The Process Coordinator manages all aspects of the Guide within that environment, including implementation and ongoing compliance.

Product—an internally or externally saleable commodity produced by an organization. A product may be a good or a service.

Product Delivery Planning—management of the delivery requirements for products generated for Consumers and Influence Management.

Project (Activity/Task) Plan Definition—the creation of a detailed and officially approved project plan may seem like additional overhead but "just getting on with it" without an agreed-upon project plan to monitor progress often leads to the "forget about that and get on with something else" syndrome. Once that happens the project fades into oblivion—or at least until management asks for an update.

Release of Fully Qualified Work Packages—once the detailed plan has been completed, the work packages may be released. The Fully Qualified Work Packages are the definitive cost accumulators and should feed back to the project and business plan for management of the project and monitoring of costs.

Role—is the name and description of a job. It is not an official organization title.

Scope Creep—is the propensity for a project to become bigger than originally contracted. It usually occurs because the original proposal, not thought through, expands out of control.

Scope Crimp—the result of the implementation team spending so much time and money to ensure that scope creep and blame will not occur that there is not enough time or money remaining to implement the original scope of the project. In situations like this, portions of the original scope move to the infamous "Phase 1," a contrivance usually included on the Risk and Issues Log.

Shelf-Ware—software or software modules/capabilities not installed or otherwise implemented even though purchased for good reason. More often than not, this software leads to ongoing maintenance fee payments and often required maintenance to assure software supplier contract compliance.

Solution Center (sometimes called a Conference Room Pilot)—the equivalent of a live operational environment where the team and consumers validate applications, processes, etc., before full implementation of concepts in a live environment in order to assure the desired effect on the business.

Sponsor—is the ECM Guide manager and driver.

Stakeholder—is the person usually responsible for a Business or Function Scenario(s). Stakeholders are members of the implementation management team and continue as part of the ongoing compliance team. Process Coordinator(s) report to Stakeholders.

Work Commissioning—the successful accomplishment of the required task. Sometimes, one portion of the work may seem to be operating correctly but when integrated with the balance of the work, the total becomes a poor performer. This happens frequently when dealing with software or process-related projects. The creation and use of a Conference Room Pilot during the Design (Create) Management phase often assists in overcoming this problem.

Work Management—all work packages require some form of detailed management, if only to check the completion of the work and the necessary information gathered. If the work package entails a significant amount of effort and/or costly resources, then attention to progressive detail should be required.

Work Package/Project Creation—is the creation and authorization of work packages and/or projects to carry out the strategic plan as modified by the constraints of the investment plan.

0-595-32372-3

www.ingramcontent.com/pod-product-compliance
Lightning Source LLC
Chambersburg PA
CBHW030907180526